How to ⸱  ......ᵧ

from Ruining Your Life

33 Methods for Women to Defeat Anxiety, Negative Thoughts, Worry, Stress, and Panic Attacks

Table of Contents

Section 1: Defining and explaining what overthinking is, where it comes from, and how deeply it can affect your life.

Section 2: Methods to defeat overthinking.

Just For You!

A FREE GIFT TO OUR READERS

40 printable and audio affirmations to help you calm your mind daily. Visit this link:

www.tinyurl.com/helencorbyn

Introduction

We are dying from overthinking. We are slowly killing ourselves by thinking about everything. Think. Think. Think. You can never trust the human mind anyway. It is a death trap. –Anthony Hopkins

I want to begin with a wake-up call to you, my dear reader; you may be killing yourself slowly without even realizing it. Our minds are so powerful that we do not even recognize when we are allowing our thoughts to control our entire lives. We devote much of our time thinking about what defines us as people, our past experiences, feelings, deepest desires, and hopes for the future. Many of us try our best to avoid thinking so much about all these aspects of life because we are afraid of what our thoughts will reveal. There is a specific group of women who live inside their heads and are consumed by their thoughts. Their minds have become enslaved to replaying past mistakes or inflicted with uncertainty and stress over the future. This specific group is known as the overthinkers. Overthinking is not an uncommon human characteristic; yes, we all tend to overthink, especially women. Perhaps it is the presentation you must give to your work department on Tuesday. Alternatively, maybe it was your argument with your spouse the week before. Perhaps you missed your best friend's birthday party, or you said something that you now regret saying. The list of things that we can overthink is endless.

Thinking about things is good, but it can develop into a toxic, harmful habit that can cause great harm. I'm going to ask you some questions; however, I want you to be as honest as you can with yourself when answering, as this is the only way to see real growth. It begins with honest self-reflection. How often do you find yourself up at night worrying over something that happened during the day? Whenever you are faced with a choice, do you second-guess yourself constantly before making a final decision? Do you feel overwhelmed by your thoughts? Do you constantly worry about your children to the point that it gives you anxiety? How much time in your day is spent worrying about things that already occurred or may occur later on? If your answer to all or any of these questions is a genuine yes, this book is meant for you. As you may be aware, overthinking can become quite exhausting. If only you knew how many problems you create for yourself that could be solved if you could stop overthinking right in its tracks. I want to take advantage of this moment to remind you that you are not alone.

The next bit of information I want to share is that it is natural for all human beings to spend time thinking. Research has proven that "the average person typically has more than 6000 thoughts in a single day" (Murdock, 2020). It sounds like a lot, doesn't it? As excessive as this may seem, overthinking has nothing to do with how many thoughts you have but rather the quality of your thoughts. Overthinking is characterized by negative thoughts and can become very dangerous when you frequently repeat these negative thoughts. Indeed, overthinking has the power to cripple every one of us when we are not aware of how it can affect us. What makes overthinking even more problematic, especially in today's society, is that it has become such a prevalent and accepted trend that far too many women overlook their tendency to overthink.

Have you ever heard of the legendary magician Harry Houdini? Indeed, a name so popular and well known for his magical tricks could not fall prey to overthinking, right? Although Houdini has been recognized for his ability to escape any jail cell he was locked in, there was one cell he was never able to escape—his mind. Houdini's claim of being able to escape any jail cell became so immensely popular that a prison in the South invited him to perform his feat of escaping their cell. He confidently accepted the challenge, and on the scheduled day, he marched into the cell as the doors closed behind him. A vast crowd gathered to watch his feat. He began his escape routine by removing his coat and his belt. His audience was unaware of the iron steel tool hidden in his belt, which he then began to use to start his escape. However, as more time passed, his confidence dwindled as he struggled to get the metal doors to open. After two hours, he realized he could not escape the prison cells and collapsed to his feet, leaning against the cell doors, which flew open. To his astonishment, the doors were never locked. His inability to unlock the prison cell doors stemmed from overthinking a very simple situation, a character flaw that far too many of us share.

Before going any further, I also want to share another story to help you understand how critical overthinking is. This story is about Julia, a recently divorced, thirty-eight-year-old single mom to her son. She is an assistant branch store manager at a local bank in her area and is hardworking, brilliant, and a loving mom. Presently there is a vacancy for promotion to branch manager at another bank in her area, and she recently interviewed with the executives for the position. For the two nights after her interview, she cannot sleep and feels like her mind is in an endless circle. Her thoughts seem never-ending, and her mind is full of unanswered questions. This cycle happens whenever she worries about her future or something that has occurred in the past. She keeps asking herself over and over, why haven't they called yet? Should I follow up with a call or an email? Perhaps the position has already been filled? Questions about if she is qualified for the position consume her mind for the entire night.

Her anxiety grows with each passing day that she does not get a response to the question of whether she has been successful or not in her interview. Although she knows a week has not passed, and it is still early, her mind refuses to leave her in peace. After much mental debate, she sends a follow-up email to the recruiters, as she feels she needs an answer. She composes the most direct yet polite message and hits send. After sending the email, her mental anguish only increases as she worries that she should have waited for a response before reaching out. We all must understand that Julia's story resonates with many of us, as it is a prime example of overthinking. Negative thinking, self-doubt, stress, and anxiety are all traits overthinkers may be very closely familiar with.

This leads us to the heart of our problem; how do we calm our minds from overthinking? The answer is not as simple as others may want to believe. We cannot simply stop thinking so much, as overthinking is an issue that runs much deeper than we realize. To get to the root of overthinking, you need to view it as a firmly rooted tree. A woodsman would find it impossible to remove a tree without cutting down its roots. This is the principle you need to apply if you want to stop overthinking at its roots; you must first understand what it is to make any changes. The overall purpose of this book is to help you become aware of how overthinking affects your life and your family and give you the tools you need to get to the root of your problem and stop overthinking.

Looking Ahead

Overthinking might have become a part of your life you do not want and desperately wish you could control. I can empathize with how difficult it is to second-guess yourself or constantly replay negative past experiences that leave you feeling stressed or anxious. You might find yourself replaying every scenario and thinking about different outcomes at night. You feel restless and always in a state of overdrive; I can empathize because I have been there with you. For far too long, I allowed overthinking to control my life, leaving me paralyzed by my anxiety. My life changed for the better when I realized the energy invested in negative thinking was not worth it. Over the years, I have dedicated myself to studying and researching more about mindsets and positive thinking. I have learned overthinking hinders our parenting, personal development, and growth, as we become obsessed with our failures or worry about potential adverse outcomes.

The more I learned about the power of thoughts; the more profound my desire grew to share this information with others, as I recognized I was not alone. Multiple conversations revealed to me that many people felt imprisoned in their minds. So, this book is my passion project to share the proven strategies and habits that helped me to overcome my overthinking. Even if you feel stuck in a cycle of constant mental warfare, I am here to encourage you and show you that you do have the power to control your thoughts. If overthinking has been a habit for as long as you can remember, this is your opportunity to learn how to counter this harmful, self-destructive habit. Excessive overthinking can create problems that never even existed, damaging your relationships with your children, family, friends, and overall life. This book will assist you in overcoming your repetitive, unhealthy thoughts and in learning how to replace them with positive, powerful thoughts that bring love, peace, and happiness into your life. It all depends on you changing your approach and the type of questions you ask yourself. By this book's end, if you apply the following methods, you will feel more confident, validated, and have better clarity in your thoughts.

Your mind is incredible, powerful, and has impressive capabilities. However, allowing negative thoughts to consume you becomes a breeding ground for anxiety, stress, confusion, and even depression. Until you can master the art of taking control of your thoughts and thinking responsibly, you may never be able to have the mental peace you desire. When you overthink, it results in a feeble mind, a mind that blocks all potential opportunities for happiness. As the story of Houdini highlighted above, the only door that is truly closed is the one that we close in our minds. I will show you how to reopen the mental doors that overthinking has closed for you. This is your chance to reclaim control over the quality of your thoughts. It is time to learn the necessary skills and habits to help prevent your mind from spiraling into negative thoughts and overthinking. You are the only person with the power to learn more about yourself, achieve your goals, overcome your fears, and work towards achieving your dreams. The key is to decide what words you repeat to yourself, as this can either limit you or place you on a path towards success. Overthinking prevents you from choosing your own story, but you can create a different story.

What to Expect in This Book

The chapters in this book are a thorough guide that will teach you about the root of overthinking and how to improve your mindset. Chapter 1 begins with a discussion about what overthinking is and how it originates. Chapter 2 builds on the discussion by focusing on the harmful effects of overthinking and how to become aware of them. In chapter 3, the focus moves on to analyzing how your mindset and negative thoughts hold you back from transforming your life. Chapter 4 is where you will learn strategies to help you to control and fight back against overthinking. Techniques to improve your focus and stop overthinking are the main discussion points in chapter 5. In chapters 6 and 7, you will learn how loving yourself and being accountable will help you overcome overthinking. I believe this book will be the answer you have been searching for, as I have ensured that no stones are left unturned as you begin your healing process.

Throughout this book, I will provide relatable stories and exercises that will allow you to understand the power of self-reflection. In each chapter, the information provided will allow you to reflect on who you are as a woman, and identify what you would like to achieve in your life. The methods provided will help you formulate your personal long-term plan to overcome the factor that keeps you back called overthinking. As you embark on this journey, I want you to reflect on the things you overthink that you would like to change. Your results will depend on how honest you are with yourself and the amount of effort you are willing to put in.

You may notice in the beginning, you feel doubtful, and you might even begin to overthink the journey that you have now started. Relax for a moment, as this is an entirely normal reaction and a positive sign that you are taking a step in the right direction. I recommend creating a personal notebook or journal to record notes and things you discover about yourself. I provide a few pages in the back of this book for notes as well. Your notebook will be your private and personal safe space for reflection and help you stay committed to your journey. Above all, you must be patient and remember that change is coming your way. You decided to read this book as you wanted nothing more than to work on one of the best factors about your life, *yourself.* I am glad you chose me to proceed on this journey with you. I am here for you, and I know that by the end of this book, you will be even better at thinking positively and enjoying your life. Now without much further ado, if you are ready to learn about the roots of overthinking, let us begin!

Section 1: Defining and Explaining What Overthinking is, Where it Comes From, and How Deeply it Can Affect Your Life.

Chapter 1: Discovering the Roots of Overthinking

Do not get too deep; it leads to overthinking, and overthinking leads to problems that don't exist in the first place. –Jayson Engay

If you had to define the concept of overthinking, what are some words that would immediately come to your mind? Although there are a variety of applicable definitions for the term, the one that stood out to me perfectly encapsulated how harmful overthinking can be. By definition, to overthink means "to think about something; to put too much time into thinking about or analyzing something in a way that is more harmful than helpful" (*Definition of OVERTHINK*, n.d.). Overthinking can appear as rumination; as Anderson Witmer (2021) explains, "you repetitively dwell on the same thought or situation over and over to the point it gets in the way of your life. Overthinking usually falls under two categories: ruminating about the past or worrying about the future." Moore (2015) adds to the discussion by explaining that "rumination consists of both brooding and a reflection component in which brooding involves repetitive dwelling on unfavorable outcomes whereas reflection involves information-seeking to better understand one's distress." This form of ruminating or overthinking has one final result—stress, as you may find it difficult to concentrate on something other than your thoughts.

If you find yourself lying awake at night and unable to sleep because you are replaying events in your mind, wondering if you spent enough time with your children throughout the day, or worrying about tomorrow, then you are overthinking and not alone. Research shows that "68% of adults admit to overthinking" (Charlie, 2022). Another study revealed that "overthinking is especially problematic for young to middle-aged adults. 73% of 23-35-year-olds and 52% of those aged 45-55 overthink" (Charlie, 2022). That is quite a vast number that many may find shocking. So, the question now stands: precisely what are people overthinking? There are so many things (especially for the age groups reflected in the findings) that people overthink. Issues such as finances or relationships are generally the first two topics that come to mind, but what other things are there? Single people may find themselves overthinking what things they should discuss on a date, what to wear, where to go, or even what type of first impression they give. Charlie (2022) explains that some of the more common things people tend to overthink include how to change social plans or hidden clues and meanings from a WhatsApp message. Perhaps you sent someone a message, and they did not respond immediately or return your call, or something as significant as saying "I love you" for the first time could be one of the many things people overthink.

Understanding the Personality Traits of an Overthinker

We must face it; overthinking happens to us all. At first, it may appear completely harmless, as it may seem like you are just spending time alone with your thoughts, right? The issue arises when your thoughts increase and transition from a positive note to a negative note, which results in feelings of self-doubt, and, even worse, feelings of anxiety and depression. This is where overthinking can become extremely dangerous and affects your mental health, as your mind becomes exhausted from the constant worrying. One of the first steps towards understanding the impact of overthinking is recognizing that you are doing it. So, here are some warning signs that can help you to identify when you are overthinking:

- You notice it is extremely difficult to stop worrying.
- You begin to worry about things that you have no control over.
- You remind yourself constantly of past mistakes.
- You replay embarrassing moments over and over in your mind.
- You constantly ask yourself "what if" questions regarding past events.
- You find sleeping difficult at night because you cannot stop your thoughts.
- You recall things you wish you had not said during previous conversations or think of things you wish you had said.
- You are focused on the hidden meanings of messages people have sent you.
- You dwell on the behavior of others that you do not like.
- You cannot be mindful and enjoy the present, as your mind focuses on past events.

Do any of those warning signs sound familiar to you? Apart from recognizing the warning signs of when you are overthinking, you should also be able to note how overthinking affects your personality. Overthinking can affect the quality of your relationships with your family and friends, as your mind is so fixated on your problems that you may begin to isolate yourself from others. Self-isolation due to overthinking can only lead to even more negative thoughts. Besides affecting your relationships, overthinking can make you an indecisive person. Thinking is the tool that we use to create ideas and solutions for our everyday problems. However, when overthinking becomes a destructive habit, it becomes much more challenging to focus on an individual situation to address, as multiple scenarios bog your mind down. This could increase the risk for more severe consequences, as you cannot focus on events that need your attention and may be afraid of making a decision.

Overthinking can also contribute to stifling your creativity. As human beings, we possess the unique ability to think outside of the box. However, the more energy and time you devote to replaying thoughts over and over, the more exhausted your mind becomes, leaving you unable to be as creative as you would like. Javier (2021) highlighted research conducted in the U.K. discovered that "when certain parts of your brain and cognitive processes are quiet, you are more creative. However, the mental rut caused by overthinking overrides our creative thoughts." Not only does overthinking turn you into a less creative individual, but it can also leave you feeling exhausted. Physical work is naturally exhausting. If you're a mom, you already know how exhausting raising children can be sometimes. Adding mental exhaustion to the list due to spending so much time replaying thoughts without solutions can leave you feeling drained and overwhelmed. It is stated that "mental energy without any sort of physical outlet absolutely can make it fatiguing and make it feel like you're exhausted because you spent so much time in your own head" (Javier, 2021).

Another characteristic that is usually associated with overthinking is irritability. After a long day of physical work, you probably feel uneasy and need a relaxing bath and some sleep. Adding insomnia due to overthinking at night can make you feel irritated and worsen your sleep cycle, which in the long run can negatively affect your health.

Overthinking: Women vs. Men

Although overthinking affects both men and women, studies have shown how overthinking affects women more than it affects men. It has been said that "most women overthink and overthinking leads to depression, an inability to move forward and wrecked emotional health" (UM News Service, 2003). Even more shocking is that what was initially labeled as a widely known stereotype that women overthink everything was confirmed in a study that says women overthink more than men because their brains are experiencing more activity. Women are uniquely vulnerable to overthinking situations about their children, career advancements, romantic situations, or health problems.

Overthinking is not a Mental Disorder

Now that you have a clearer picture of what overthinking is, it is essential to clarify what it is not. Overthinking is not classified as a mental health disorder. However, it is usually associated with conditions such as anxiety disorders, depression, post-traumatic stress disorder (PTSD), or obsessive-compulsive disorder (OCD). Anderson Witner (2015) describes the relationship between overthinking and our mental health as "a chicken and egg situation: High levels of stress, anxiety, and depression can contribute to overthinking. Meanwhile, overthinking may increase stress, anxiety, and depression."

What Can Trigger Overthinking?

Stress and Anxiety from Fear of the Unknown:

So, let us shake things up a little bit. We have looked at what overthinking is, some of the traits associated with overthinkers, and recognizing when you are overthinking. The next best question that I suppose you may ponder is, "what can trigger overthinking?" It is essential to understand that one of the leading causes of overthinking is stress. We identified earlier that although overthinking is not classified as a mental disorder, it is linked to feelings of anxiety or PTSD. Stress is a normal part of our lives, as we all experience life events that leave us feeling stressed or anxious over what is about to happen next in our lives. Felman (2020) explains that "stress is a natural feeling of not being able to cope with specific demands and events." Felman also clarifies that "these demands can come from work, relationships, financial pressures, and other situations, but anything that poses a real or perceived challenge or threat to a person's well-being can cause stress." Although stress is normal, it can result in you overthinking even more about what caused you to feel stressed in the first place.

Depression:

Research indicates that "depressed individuals often overthink or ruminate about their problems and distressing feelings" (Moore, 2015). What sets people who are depressed apart from others is how they think and feel about themselves, others, and their surrounding environments. To understand the difference in outlook, you should be able to define what depression is. A clear definition of the term explains that "depression is a dysfunctional disorder that involves avoidance, withdrawal, and inactivity in one's social environment" (Moore, 2015). When someone feels depressed over their circumstances, they usually resort to constantly replaying the factors in their mind that have contributed to their depressed state. This can lead to even more severe health issues, as the longer someone overthinks about the factors contributing to their depression, the more severe their depression will become.

Perfectionism:

Perfectionism is a concept that goes hand in hand with overthinking but is often misunderstood in terms of what it means. Perfectionism is not based on your ability to be perfect but on feeling perfect. People have difficulty expressing their thoughts about a particular issue or situation because they do not feel perfect about it. We encounter this idea of feeling perfect almost every single day. Overthinking and perfectionism are usually why most people procrastinate and avoid starting new tasks. It could be something simple like changing your diet or starting your own business. Perfectionism encourages the overthinker to believe in the excuse that they are taking the time to think about it some more. However, the real dark secret behind perfectionism is not the need for more time but instead being driven by a fear of failure. People use perfectionism as a shield to avoid taking blame or judgment for their mistakes.

Perfectionism can trigger overthinking negatively. You can become paralyzed by your desire to achieve perfection when you overthink. Vice versa, when your need for perfection controls you, you begin to overthink your actions. For example, imagine your manager asks you to send out a brief memo to staff in your department reminding them about the upcoming fundraiser. As you begin to type the memo, you think of what words to use to ensure it reads perfectly. The more you type, the more you realize that it does not feel perfect, and it results in you taking more than forty minutes trying to perfect a paragraph that should have only taken about five minutes. It then leads to feelings of frustration and even more stress. It is also helpful to note that perfectionism leads to the traits of overthinking that we discussed earlier, feeling indecisive, and lacking creativity. We will discuss perfectionism in greater detail a little later on.

Getting to the Root:

Now that we have covered the triggers of overthinking, let us discuss in more detail the causes of overthinking. It helps to label the causes you are about to learn as the roots of overthinking. You did not just wake up one day and decide that overthinking would become a daily habit. We are born into this unique world as children with primarily blank slates. Our thoughts and beliefs are learned or passed on to us as we age. I can think of many sayings that you may have heard over the years, such as:

"You need an education to be successful."

"You need to lose weight because being fat is not beautiful."

"Nobody will ever love someone like you."

All possible negative thoughts get passed on by the people closest to you. Their beliefs eventually become your reality. When you begin to overthink, one of the main reasons is that your mind replays the limiting beliefs that have become rooted in your subconscious. Let us take a closer look at how we learn to overthink due to external factors in our lives.

Trauma, Inherited or Generational:

Many of us have experienced a traumatic event, such as an accident or losing a loved one, which can cause us to become hypervigilant. When you experience any form of trauma, the side effect is that your mind goes into a state of constant high alert. You are always looking for real or perceived threats, as you are stuck in fight or flight response mode. People who have experienced traumatic events, such as a near-death vehicular accident, are more prone to overthinking. Unfortunately, some of us, as kids, had to grow up dealing with difficult or frightening situations, which led to overthinking being integrated as a daily habit.

A perfect example would be to look at the child who had to grow up with an alcoholic parent who became abusive when drunk. It is easy to understand why a child might spend time replaying certain events constantly and worrying about what they can do to avoid their alcoholic parent. Overthinking will generally become a safety net that develops as they get older. Likewise, because our parents are our first role models and responsible for nurturing us and teaching values, growing up with family members who overthink contributes to overthinking as a learned behavior. Have you ever heard the saying that you become what you see? This concept can be applied to overthinking, as you can inherit a behavior if you grow up in an environment where it frequently happens.

Having an Illusion of Control:

Being placed in a situation where you feel out of control and helpless is one of the most challenging things to go through in life. These moments happen often, and the only way to make sense of what is happening around you is to spend time scrutinizing every detail of the situation. Overthinking can develop a false sense of security and the belief that you have control over a situation. You feel more certain about your decisions because, in your mind, you think about every possible outcome. I am sure you would agree that most people hate feeling helpless and would do anything to have the power to either help themselves or assist a loved one. Even if we are genuinely unable to change a situation, overthinking can give the illusion that we can execute change. Overthinking feels more helpful and keeps that feeling of being helpless at bay.

Fear of Conflict:

I have never met anyone who truly enjoys conflict or confrontation, have you? Arguments result in negative emotions that many want to avoid feeling, so they actively look for ways to prevent any situations in which conflict can arise. Whenever a confrontation occurs, the person involved can feel less confident about their ability to handle the situation. This can cause overthinking, as more time is devoted to thinking of ways to avoid any adverse situation.

Positive Uses of Overthinking:

So far, you may read everything I have shared and immediately start wondering, is everything about overthinking destructive or harmful? I want to be the bearer of good news and inform you that there is a silver lining to overthinking. The issue is, and this will be the primary focus of the rest of this book when overthinking shifts to dwelling only on your negative thoughts, which ultimately influence your outlook on your life. Despite the associated negative factors, overthinking can positively help decision-making, solving problems, and feeling more creative. I want to reassure you that overthinking is okay, as long as you are aware of the direction in which your thoughts are going. Taking the time to identify the trigger behind your overthinking, whether you are thinking from a zone of anxiety or an abundance zone, will determine if you are overthinking for a positive outcome.

Decision Making:

We have analyzed how overthinking can result in procrastination or feeling indecisive. However, in some instances, postponing the decision process can be a positive rather than a negative outcome. When you delay making a decision, it gives you more time to select the best option possible. It also allows you to reflect on when you may have failed and think of ways to avoid repeating your past mistakes. In this context, reflection becomes a critical component of your thinking process, as the objective turns to identify a way forward instead of ruminating or dwelling on your past failures.

Overcoming Lack of Creativity and Solving Problems:

Overthinking can stifle your creativity, and when you dwell too much on the negative, it leaves you stuck in your problem instead of solving it. However, there can be scenarios where spending more time analyzing the situation can help you think of new and innovative ways to solve your problems. It also provides a unique opportunity for others to get involved in decision-making. As a result, more input can contribute to a more enriched and positive output.

Chapter Reflection

So, there we have it, the beginning of our analysis of what overthinking is, the triggers, causes, or roots of overthinking. Overthinking is a specific style of thought in which your worries become a never-ending cycle. This endless cycle can overwhelm you with stress, anxiety, or fear. In some cases, overthinking can be harmless and even result in positive outcomes such as improved decision-making, problem-solving, and becoming a more creative person. In most contexts, overthinking or ruminating can result in you feeling paralyzed or debilitated because your mind is repeatedly replaying your negative thoughts. You feel stuck, as the problem you are thinking about remains unsolved due to your spiraling negative thoughts. To begin the process of overcoming overthinking, you need to identify what triggered you to resort to overthinking. Apart from understanding your triggers, the next stage is to understand the factors that caused you to continue to overthink as a habit in your present. These factors are the foundation or the root causes of your overthinking.

The roots of overthinking can run deep. Perhaps you have tried to break free from overthinking before, and it did not seem to work out the way you had envisioned. It could be that you viewed overthinking at the surface level, as opposed to taking a closer look at the roots, the deeper reasons for your overthinking habit. I want you to view overthinking as a firmly planted tree that needs to be chopped down. In order to figure out what tools are needed to start removing the tree, you need to be aware of the tree's roots. In this chapter, I started you off by identifying the roots of overthinking, and now you are ready to move on to the next phase of overcoming overthinking. In the following chapter, you will learn about the depths of overthinking and how to avoid being stuck in a place called "the Dwell Well."

Chapter 2: Become Aware, but Don't Get Stuck in the Dwell Well

Nothing can harm you as much as your own thoughts unguarded. –Buddha

This chapter is a continuation of the principles of overthinking that you were introduced to in chapter 1. We began with an introductory look at the root causes of overthinking and how to recognize the warning signs of when you are overthinking. One of the emerging issues is that not everyone is entirely aware of the depth to which overthinking is affecting their lives. Most of the negative situations that we experience in our lives occur as a result of overthinking. Still, not all of us can relate the consequences we are now experiencing to our ruminating or worrying. The first method of stopping overthinking right in its tracks is to become aware of exactly how it is affecting you. Awareness is a powerful tool that leads to change, allowing you to manage your thoughts better. As you become more aware and mindful of the quality of your thoughts, it can help you avoid becoming stuck in a place that I like to call "the Dwell Well."

If you recall, rumination refers to repetitively dwelling on past unfavorable outcomes. The more you meditate or dwell on your past, the more it can make you feel like you are falling into a deep well. Your negative thoughts become so powerful that they leave you feeling like you are stuck at the bottom of this well, with no means of escape. This leads us to the goal of this chapter, to help you become aware of the extent to which overthinking controls you before you spiral downwards and become trapped in your Dwell Well. It is possible to be completely aware of how overthinking has affected you. You can use this awareness to motivate you and not dwell on your experiences to the point where you feel stuck with no way out. If you are ready to open your mind, let us proceed.

The Negative Effects of Overthinking:

Your mind is the most powerful and unique tool that you possess, but did you know that that tool can work against you? Your mind is a gift that ultimately controls and shapes the outcome of your entire life, as it contains all your emotions and thoughts. However, when negative thoughts or feelings bog your mind down, that gift could turn into an uncomfortable experience and possibly be detrimental to your health. My conclusions about the harmful effects of overthinking come from the research I've conducted over the years and conversations that

I've had with both women and men about their life experiences. I have discovered that:

• overthinking contributes to making your life harder. When you overthink, the stressful factors you face are magnified and appear more significant than they truly are. The more stressed you feel, the more difficult it becomes to find an effective solution for your problems, and you are also more likely to react to your stress negatively and intensely.

• overthinking can damage your relationships because it can trigger unnecessary arguments and conflicts, and the overthinker may not understand what is needed on their part to help improve the relationship.

• overthinking is one of the primary contributing factors to mental health disorders, including anxiety and depression.

The Most Dangerous Effects: Paralysis, Depression, Anxiety, and Insomnia:

Paralysis:

In this context, paralysis refers to your inability to make decisions because of fear of overthinking. What is stopping you from making decisions? It is because your mind focuses on analyzing the multiple ways a scenario could turn out, mostly negative, which leaves you paralyzed and afraid to come to a final decision. Take, for example, the entrepreneur who wants to launch their restaurant, but they keep overthinking about what could go wrong if they were to start their own business. They think about whether sales will be slow, or they worry about finding the perfect location for their business. This fear of what could go wrong leaves them paralyzed and stuck and ultimately prevents them from taking any action to launch their career.

Depression:

Overthinking or ruminating about past events is usually the leading cause of depression in many people. The very core of depression is based on repeating negative experiences and reliving these moments frequently in your mind, which results in feelings of misery, anger, and sadness. Perhaps you have heard others remark they keep thinking about how things could have been if they had done something or acted differently, dwelling on alternative scenarios and "what if" statements is unhealthy and allows you to remain depressed. It is important to remember that you cannot change your past, and overthinking about things you are unable to change is the root of depression.

Losing a loved one can also result in depression due to grief. My research on the subject has led me to discover that people who overthink frequently are at a higher risk of developing depression due to losing a loved one. I have read about many women who have suffered the loss of a relative or close friend due to a terminal illness, the main reason being cancer. Their experiences have been heartbreaking, to say the least; they have sunk into severe depression as they couldn't stop ruminating on how to rebuild their lives without the person they had just lost. Other stories I have encountered reveal the concerns of many whose friends couldn't understand why they simply could not get over losing someone they were close to. I learned a lot from these personal stories that were shared with me, specifically how stable the state of depression can be due to overthinking.

I want to share a story to give you a better context. I will share Roxanne's story of how overthinking affected her life after losing her sister, Lisa, to breast cancer. Lisa and Roxanne were very close as children and were only separated in age by one year. As they transitioned into adulthood, they remained very close and became each other's sources of emotional support. When Lisa was diagnosed at thirty-four with breast cancer, they promised each other that they would remain positive and fight the battle together. However, whenever Roxanne was not in the company of her sister, she found herself worrying about her sister's diagnosis, she lost sleep, was unable to eat, and her rumination resulted in her feeling depressed. She kept asking herself; what would she do without her sister? Why couldn't it have been her instead?

Unfortunately, tragedy struck, and Lisa succumbed to her illness, despite receiving the best possible treatment. Like many, after losing a loved one, Roxanne was shocked and isolated herself from the company of others. As the days passed, her overthinking increased, and she replayed conversations she'd had with her sister or analyzed whether the doctors had done enough to take care of her sister. In Roxanne's situation, you can observe that overthinking helped to prolong her feelings of grief over losing someone she loved. This situation can make depression even more severe, as overthinking leaves you feeling stuck in a place of pain and sadness.

Anxiety:

It is natural to feel anxious over events in our lives. In the United States, it is recorded that approximately forty million people suffer from anxiety (Anxiety and Depression Association of America, 2019). Increased stress only results in heightened levels of anxiety. Anxiety is linked to the nature of your thoughts and emotions, in that when your thoughts are harmful, it also creates negative emotions such as anger or fear. When you become plagued by these negative emotions, for instance, worrying about your future, it makes it harder for you to enjoy being in the present. Anxiety can leave you feeling mentally drained and miserable. The more anxious you feel, the more you tend to overthink, which can result in depression, or, even worse, thoughts of suicide. I want you to recall this book's first opening sentence; you can overthink yourself to death.

Insomnia:

I am sure you were laid in bed at some point, exhausted and desperately craving the peace of sleep, yet your mind remained restless and refused to shut down. How often do you feel physically tired, but your thoughts are nonstop and keeping you up? Insomnia occurs when your mind becomes tired from overthinking. There is a section of our brain known as the hippocampus responsible for our short-term memories, which can be affected by overthinking. When the hippocampus becomes affected, it also affects the responses sent to your body's nervous system. What occurs is an increase in the stress hormone known as cortisol, which helps to coordinate your sleep cycle. Too much cortisol consequently results in insomnia. This is why it is essential to recognize the role of overthinking, as it can devastate your physical and mental health.

Other Negative Effects:

The above four named effects are considered some of the most critical and dangerous impacts of overthinking, but they are not the only effects. Several physical effects can occur from excessive rumination or overthinking that have not been considered yet. One of the first effects is that you can become less imaginative and inventive. Studies have found that you imagine more when specific areas of your mind are at peace. Overthinking disrupts your psychological process, causing a mental block that prevents you from thinking of new ideas. Apart from a decrease in creativity and invention, you may also feel less energetic due to overthinking. Overthinking requires a ton of mental energy, which can result in you feeling depleted and exhausted because all your energy has been spent on thinking and worrying too much.

Overthinking and Relationships:

By now, you should have a clearer picture of how overthinking can seriously impact your life in terms of your physical and mental health. But have you ever stopped to consider how overthinking can affect your relationships? It may come as a surprise to many, but overthinking is one of the primary reasons for the breakdown or destruction of a relationship. Not only applying to romantic or intimate relationships but friendships, family, and work relationships as well. I've heard a question: "how can overthinking contribute to destroying a relationship?" How does overthinking lead to the destruction of an otherwise healthy relationship? To put things into better perspective, I want you to think of someone you love and admire deeply. Over time you have developed a relationship built on trust and genuine love, yet despite how well you have grown to know and love this person, your mind is telling you to doubt the bond that both of you share. You begin to worry and constantly ask yourself questions such as:

- "Is this relationship going to last?"
- "Do they truly love me for me or are they hiding something from me?"
- "Am I truly deserving of a loving relationship, or would they leave me for someone better?"

These negative thoughts continue to control your mind and ultimately lead to sabotaging behavior such as an increase in arguments or pushing your partner away. Even though your actions are not done purposefully, your overthinking has resulted in a type of worrying known as relationship anxiety. Relationship anxiety is characteristic of intense feelings of doubt and insecurity over your relationship. You find yourself overthinking whether you are indeed important, and you doubt the compatibility between yourself and your partner. Overthinking the legitimacy of your relationship only results in a loss of trust in the connection and its ultimate breakdown. Although this example applies to a romantic relationship, the same principle of doubting the legitimacy of a relationship by overthinking can apply to any other relationship category. Overthinking in your relationships only creates non-existent problems, makes it difficult for trust to be established, and in the long-term, it can affect your mental health as you find it challenging to maintain healthy, supportive relationships.

I want to talk about Andrea's story for a minute as I believe that sharing her story with you may help you feel less alone when it comes to overthinking in relationships. Andrea had everything a person could ask for regarding her outward appearance—a loving boyfriend, a successful and stable career, and a handful of friends. What many did not know about Andrea was that on the inside, she felt as if her doubts and thoughts were on a rollercoaster that would never end. She would find herself questioning every little detail. Was she too possessive? What was her boyfriend doing during that hour when he was too busy to respond to her messages? Even though he never gave her any reason to question his loyalty, Andrea often doubted his sincerity and commitment to their relationship, which resulted in many heated arguments. I choose to highlight Andrea's story as this isn't an abnormal occurrence. Many women and men are like her, questioning every detail of their relationships. The issue is that many people cannot recognize when they are overthinking and genuinely believe that their doubts and fears are rational.

Are You Overthinking It? Quiz:

You must learn to recognize when you are overthinking, as awareness is your most powerful weapon if you want to quit overthinking as a habit. When you feel sad or nervous, for example, have you ever taken the time to observe your response? I want to provide a brief quiz that I find helpful for evaluating if you tend to overthink and become stuck, dwelling on your negative thoughts. This is the perfect time to take out that notebook I advised you to start at the beginning of this journey and record your answers for the scenarios described below.

Your response should be *never*, *sometimes*, or *always* for each listed situation. To answer each scenario, think about a time when you felt upset or angry, and reflect on whether the scenario described applies to you.

• I feel as if I am alone.
• I feel fatigued.

- I find it difficult to concentrate, and I cannot stop thinking about how unmotivated I feel.

- I keep replaying the situation repeatedly and wishing things had gone differently.

- I keep thinking about how anxious or sad I feel.

- I think about my mistakes, faults, and shortcomings.

- I keep asking myself, "why am I unable to handle things in a much better way?"

Suppose your answer to most or all of the scenarios is *never*. In that case, I want to congratulate you, as you may have created your winning combination for overcoming overthinking.

If your answers are mostly *always* or *sometimes*, then it is possible that you are prone to excessive overthinking and can spiral out of control. This is still great news, as you have identified your overthinking potential, and you can learn how to avoid spiraling out of control and into the Dwell Well.

Spiraling out of Control Into the Dwell Well:

Overthinking involves the mental repetition of your negative emotions and thoughts. You may find yourself replaying a recent argument with a friend. Do you wonder why they would have said those things to you or what they meant when they said that? However, overthinking questions only leads to the creation of more questions. Your negative thoughts expand and take up the majority of space in your mind. At first, your thoughts may be about a scenario, but then they can transform into thinking about other events in your life or questions about your future. These questions become more negative as time goes by. You may confuse overthinking with worrying, but it is more than just dwelling on things that have already occurred. As an overthinker, your level of worry increases so drastically that you automatically feel something terrible has already happened, even before anything has taken place.

When I reflect on some of the conversations I've had as part of my research on overthinking, I find that many people have labeled overthinking as deep thinking and getting in touch with their emotions. The issue with this point of view is that when you overthink, you primarily examine your life from negative emotions, which provide a distorted view of your world. Your negative mindset only allows you to see the adverse events of your past or possible negative events in your future, not the positive ones that can occur. Your thoughts influence your emotions, so if you only think negatively, your feelings are also harmful. Your overthinking can become the leading cause of your anxiety or any other negative emotion.

The Role of Emotions:

Before we continue, I want to take a moment to remind you that you are not alone. It may feel overwhelming at first to confront your overthinking and recognize how it has affected you. I believe, however, that there is strength in numbers, so many women out there feel stressed, drained, and struggle to accept that their thoughts are affecting their emotional responses. The good thing about becoming aware of your overthinking habit is that it is the first step that you need to begin the process of transforming your thoughts. Perhaps you are not mindful of how your overthinking results in you acting upon your negative emotions. For example, you should have a lunch date with a friend who does not show up for your date. You become angry and send a message voicing your frustration over being stood up, labeling them as a bad friend, and you decide to avoid them. On the drive home, you find yourself replaying the event repeatedly in your mind, which leads to further feelings of frustration, and you may even take your anger out on someone else.

It is important to recognize when you are dwelling on an issue, as this can help you to avoid becoming stuck in the Dwell Well. The more you overthink, the more power you give to your negative emotions, which results in you feeling as if you are spiraling downwards and can ultimately leave you feeling trapped by your emotions. The best thing you can do for yourself to avoid feeling stuck is to be patient with yourself and know that change is possible. You must understand what triggered your emotion and why it affects you. Therefore, we are all emotional beings and can't avoid negative feelings, but we can control how we respond to emotions. Pay attention to how you react and what type of thoughts further influence your actions—becoming aware of how your overthinking affects you should become your first motivation for change and, ultimately, will determine how to transform your thinking.

Chapter Reflection

Even though overthinking can be a natural human response to a situation you face, it can become toxic and damage your health. Overthinking diminishes your ability to make the best decisions for yourself and stifles your creativity. It can drag your mood down, leave you to deal with anxiety and depression, and cause sleep loss, leaving you feeling paralyzed. We all need to learn how to break free of the habit of overthinking and avoid becoming stuck in a downward spiral. We can develop strategies to help overcome overthinking, but change can only begin when you become aware of the depth to which overthinking is affecting you. When you can identify how it has affected you, it can motivate you to determine the best ways to manage it. In the following chapter, we will learn to stop overthinking by shifting our mindsets.

Chapter 3: Getting Started: Do the Inner Work to Shift Your Mindset

My father taught me not to overthink things, that nothing will ever be perfect, so just keep moving and do your best. –Scott Eastwood

You've reached the stage of your journey where you are ready to begin the process to stop overthinking and prevent yourself from spiraling into that dreaded Dwell Well that we discussed in the previous chapter. Your first thoughts, I expect, will be, "so how do I get started?" The main point that has been highlighted so far is the role of negative thinking. You can enjoy freedom from overthinking if you train your mind to think positively. In this chapter, I will share strategies to make changing your mindset your priority. Your mindset is one of the tools you need for true transformation and enjoying more peace in your life. You need to ask yourself, "what does transformation look like for you?" Now that you know how negative thinking/overthinking affects you, how does it make you feel? Take a moment to record your honest reflections in your journal and use these to motivate you as you begin the process of shifting your mindset.

Mindset Matters:

Of course, we must all recognize that transforming your mindset does not occur overnight. It is a lengthy process, but I want to encourage and remind you that you have the power. It is ultimately your choice to do the inner work that is required. Perhaps you feel as if something is keeping you back from changing your negative thoughts. You want to, but you think something is in your way. If so, you must learn what mental blocks are and how they relate to your mindset. Your mindset matters the most because if you are not doing the inner work to change the nature of your thoughts, then being aware of how overthinking affects you will become useless. Self-awareness is most powerful when combined effectively with your dedication to self-improvement. Adapting to a positive outlook is essential for personal development. To ensure that your personal growth and development are successful, we will discuss how mental blocks and limiting beliefs can hinder your progress.

Understanding Mental Blocks and Limiting Beliefs:

Let us dive right in and begin with getting a better understanding of what a mental block is. If you've struggled to think clearly despite your best attempts at any point in time, then you are not alone. Most likely, you were experiencing a mental block at that moment, a mental barrier that prevents or stifles your productivity, creativity, and overall motivation. Have you ever heard of the saying "writer's block?" Even I, during the production of this book, had moments where I had trouble with finding the perfect words to illustrate my points. To put your mind at ease, writer's block doesn't only affect writers but can happen to any of us. It could happen at any given moment and hinder your ability to make simple decisions quickly.

The next question generally asked is, "what causes these phenomena, known as mental blocks?" Well, it is interesting to note that there are a variety of reasons accredited to why we experience mental blocks. Moore (2019) indicates in her research that over-the-counter medications, a lack of vitamin B12, and insomnia all contribute to mental blockage. These reasons, however, are mere slivers of the full scope of factors that can lead to a mental block. Another factor contributing to a mental block is when you feel mentally exhausted from being required to make multiple decisions, otherwise known as decision fatigue. In addition to being overwhelmed by the responsibility of making so many decisions, being placed in a cluttered environment increases cortisol production, leaving you feeling anxious and mentally overwhelmed.

Limiting Beliefs:

Similar to mental blocks, your beliefs can also hinder your ability to change your mindset. When you think about the goals you have for yourself, have you ever paid attention to why you haven't been able to achieve them? Or, when you spend so much time in your head ruminating or overthinking, saying to yourself phrases such as:

- "I will never find the job of my dreams."
- "I will never be the mom I really want to be."
- "I do not deserve to be happy or successful."

Repeating phrases such as the above over and over to yourself illustrates what is known as limiting beliefs. We create mental excuses as to why we cannot achieve our goals. Having these ideas forces you to remain stuck in your comfort zone and hinders your professional and personal development. Overthinking these negative thoughts instead of more optimistic thoughts is what will ultimately prevent you from living the life you truly want. It would be best if you did not feel dismayed, as limiting beliefs serve a purpose in our lives. They usually appear as our defense mechanism when trying to avoid feeling disappointed, frustrated, or like a failure.

Overcoming Mental Blocks and Limiting Beliefs:

So, here is the real challenge; how can you overcome your mental blocks and limiting beliefs? Building on the principle of awareness that we discussed in the previous chapter, the first step begins with identifying what triggered your block and your beliefs. Although it may seem difficult initially, you can train your mind to look at situations from a different and more positive angle instead of a negative standpoint. Here are some valuable strategies that you can implement into your daily activities to help shift your mindset:

1. Personal development must become a priority.

Your mindset will not change overnight; therefore, it is your responsibility to set aside time to work on yourself. You can try praying about it, meditating daily or visualizing the changes you want to see in your life. The goal must always be to remain committed and stick to a schedule to strengthen your mind.

2. Train your mind to observe positive changes every day.

It is easy to get caught up in only observing the negative environment that surrounds you and then dwelling on the environment that you are in. However, a helpful exercise would be to try and focus on at least three positive things that occur daily and analyze how small positive changes can be used as an opportunity for personal growth.

3. Set smaller tasks and take breaks.

The easiest step is to reduce your workload to avoid feeling mentally exhausted and blocks that occur because you are overwhelmed by your responsibilities and decisions. Try creating a list of things you need to do and begin with the tasks that aren't the most difficult. This will make it easier for you to observe progress and feel more motivated as you can focus on one task at a time. It is also important not to overwork yourself and to take breaks along the way. The more you try to push yourself when you feel mentally blocked, the more you focus on the mental barrier instead of the task. Breaks will help you clear your mind and allow you to look at your task from a different point of view.

Is There an Imposter in Your Mind?

Imposter syndrome is another factor that is often associated with mental blocks. It is characterized by an internal fear of others labeling you as a fraud or perceiving you as incompetent. In much simpler terms, a person experiencing imposter syndrome feels like a phony, like they do not belong, and tends to doubt or criticize their abilities. Because imposter syndrome reduces motivation and the fear that you will not live up to others' expectations, your mind finds it much more challenging to stay focused or achieve tasks. It may sound shocking, but many well-known public figures, such as Michelle Obama or Neil Armstrong, have all publicly admitted that they have experienced imposter syndrome. So, if you felt alone in this struggle before, you do not have to be anymore. Now that we have touched on imposter syndrome, I must mention one of the factors that play an incredible role in the development of imposter syndrome: perfectionism.

Are You a Perfectionist?

In this modern-day culture, perfectionism has unfortunately been accepted as a personal trait many believe in today. I am sure that growing up as a child, many of you were encouraged to do your best and set goals you would like to accomplish. Do not get me wrong; nothing is wrong with wanting to be a high achiever who constantly strives for excellence in everything they do. It should be applauded when someone can feel truly happy over their accomplishments while remaining humble enough to learn from the mistakes they made along the way. That makes perfectionism different from being a high achiever, as there is no room for errors. Perfectionists are often unforgiving of themselves, as they have an impeccably high standard they must achieve at all costs. The issue is that this standard they have set for themselves is impossible to accomplish, resulting in feeling like a failure and constant mental pressure to live up to these standards.

There is one simple, well-known fact about life that perfectionists ignore. The fact that life in its entirety is not perfect and will never be. You will never have the ability to control everything in your life and attempting to be perfect in everything sets you up for failure. As much as striving to be a better person is a positive aspect, positivity is pointless if it harms your overall well-being. A drive to be perfect can lead to feeling anxious, depressed, and mentally burning out from dwelling on how to live up to impossible expectations. Overthinking how to be perfect can ruin your life, preventing you from valuing yourself and all that you have to offer. If you are a perfectionist, you achieve much less than others because your mindset strips you of proper motivation. Perfectionists all share an inner fear of failure that prevents them from seeing all they have accomplished. However, let me take a moment to reassure each of you that it is possible to change from a perfectionist attitude. If you adopted a perfectionism mindset during childhood and into adulthood, this is your opportunity to stop perfectionism in its tracks.

Stop Perfectionism in its Tracks:

Having said all the above, let us examine some practical steps you can follow to shift from a perfectionist mindset. Pull out your progress notebook and reflect on whether you may have any perfectionist tendencies. Even if you cannot think of it all at once, any time you observe behavior in which you are pushing yourself to be perfect, make a mental note to record it. Apart from listing your tendencies, identify qualities you admire about yourself and why you admire them. Perfectionists spend a lot of time trying to improve themselves, to be much better, without stopping to appreciate their good qualities. It all comes down to overcoming perfectionism, shifting your focus away from trying to improve, and recognizing your present worth. By changing your self-talk, you will find it much easier to acknowledge your positive skills. Take a moment to reflect on what you tell yourself. Do you constantly say that you must try harder, as your best wasn't good enough? That mental voice in your head telling you to push yourself to impossible lengths needs to be silenced. Negative self-talk goes hand in hand with perfectionism. So, the next activity I want you to implement is to write down positive words that you can say to yourself every day to help you appreciate your work.

Overthinking and Control:

Earlier on, when discussing the causes or roots of overthinking, you may recall that we brought up the term illusion of control. To quickly recall, overthinking can help to create the illusion that you have control over a situation and can implement effective change because you have thought about every possible outcome. What leads to this urge or desire to have control over our lives? After all, having control over the lives we have been given is not a bad thing, but it can become detrimental when the desire to have control over everything consumes you. When your time is consumed by ruminating or thinking about taking control over every aspect of your life, it is usually linked to a more profound fear of the unknown. I encounter many people who struggle with accepting when something does not go according to plan or their circumstances changes unexpectedly. They found themselves stuck in a rut or the Dwell Well, as their time was spent replaying the situation and trying to understand how they might regain control. Can you relate to having this feeling at any point in your life? Have you ever wondered why this happens?

Apart from the fear of not knowing what comes next, the need for control is also rooted in the need for safety due to past traumatic experiences. When you experience an event that results in emotional or physical pain, it can further heighten your need to control how things occur in your life. It is easy for people who have experienced trauma also frequently to experience cognitive distortions. One such distortion is catastrophizing, in which you overthink and automatically expect the worst outcome in any situation. A traumatic history can also cause you to become a hypervigilant person who is scanning your surrounding environment for danger and frequently ruminating over potential traumatic events that can reoccur. Control over everything is your mind's defense system to avoid going through another traumatic experience. It may seem like the best defense system, but what you are doing is reliving the very same traumatic event over and over in your mind.

Taking Back Control:

Do not get me wrong; it is perfectly normal to want to establish a routine and a plan. The issue is when you create rigid plans that you dwell on and only overthink how to ensure that your plan remains predictable. I do not want to be the bearer of bad news but overthinking to establish control can turn you into what others label as a "control freak." However, if you are not aware of when you are overthinking and driven by your desire to be in control, it is possible to miss the warning signs of being too controlling. Basic warning signs usually include:

- Feeling too stressed or anxious over unexpected plan changes.

- Being a perfectionist.
- Catastrophizing about your future.

Now that we have identified that your need for control is usually because of inner fear, and it is entirely normal, the next step in shifting a controlling mindset is to learn what you can do to break this habit. In my research, I have found four effective methods to help you become less controlling. I have also implemented these steps in my life, and I can attest that they have made a difference in my mindset and how enjoyable life is. Here are the four steps for you to work on incorporating into your lifestyle, so you can watch the difference they make in your personal development.

1. Become aware of your controlling behavior. Take a moment to reflect on your behavior during stressful situations and record how you tend to react. This will assist you in anticipating situations where your controlling attitude may take control and help you to craft a different response.

2. By exploring your feelings, dig deeper into the causes behind your need to control. Begin by asking yourself, "what fears do I have, and how are they influencing my behavior?" You can also ask yourself, "are my fears coming from a rational place, or am I catastrophizing?"

3. Once you can identify the nature of your fears, you can challenge them by replacing them with more positive thoughts. For example, let's say you have been telling yourself repeatedly, "I will never get a better job, and I will always be a failure." You can challenge this thought by instead asking yourself:

- "how do I know that is going to happen?"
- "what evidence supports why I feel this way?"
- "is thinking like this helping me, or are my emotions affecting my judgment?"
- "am I including the positive aspects, or am I only focused on the negatives?"

4. Practice accepting what you cannot control. I believe that deep down inside, we are all aware that there are aspects of our lives that we will never be able to control entirely, and yet we insist on doing things to try and change that known fact. We all must come to terms with the law of acceptance. That means we must be able to tell the difference between the things we can control and what we can't and stop trying to alter the situations we have no control over.

Conflict is Nothing to Fear:

Another root cause of overthinking identified in the first chapter is the fear of conflict. Personally speaking, I have always actively tried to avoid conflict. During my research, I was surprised to learn that I am not alone, as others feel the same way I do. Most of my overthinking has been based on me constantly searching for ways to avoid any possible arguments with my spouse, family member, or coworker. I decided to get to the root of my fear when I noticed that my thoughts were starting to take control of me. I have discovered that fear of conflict usually develops during childhood. We observe how our parents and other role models express their concerns and how open they are to hearing someone else's feelings. In most cases, when you are exposed to an environment in which freedom of expression is limited, it can help to shape how willing you are to participate in conversations that others may perceive as threatening.

Whenever you are afraid of something, it is your natural response to avoid or withdraw from the source of your fear. Although withdrawal or avoidance might work temporarily, it only increases anxiety in the long term. Spending time ruminating or thinking about ways to avoid conflict is unhealthy and only leads to more anxiety. Likewise, once a disagreement or argument has already occurred, it can be mentally destructive to ruminate, replay what was said, or think of how it could have turned out differently. The goal is to understand that conflict is a natural part of all relationships, and your mindset will help you manage conflict successfully. A positive mindset will help you shift your focus to solving the problem rather than rehashing the issue repeatedly in your mind.

Chapter Reflection

In this chapter, you established a greater awareness of how overthinking affects your life and the steps needed to stop overthinking from controlling your life. Change is no easy process, but the best way to get started is to recognize the role of a negative mindset. Many of you might have picked up this book because you have tried other alternatives to stop constantly replaying negative thoughts in your mind, but you still feel stuck in your present state. The information provided in the chapter should have placed you on a more guided path of true transformation by helping you to become aware of beliefs and mental blocks that affect you. Likewise, for some of you, the need to be a perfectionist, the need for control, or a fear of conflict can also be the deeper cause of your overthinking habit that you have not been aware of. Now that you have come face to face with your inner fears and how they contribute to overthinking, it is the first step needed to get started. Only you can do the inner work of shifting your mindset. Personal development must begin with a positive mindset. Now that you are aware, it is time to fight back.

Section 2: Methods to Defeat Overthinking

Chapter 4: Fight Back - Daily Habits and Techniques

Overthinking will not empower you over things that are beyond your control. So, let it be if it is meant to be and cherish the moment. –Mahsati

When soldiers prepare to go out onto the battlefield, they must adorn themselves with body armor. Why wear a suit of armor? Wearing armor will make the difference between life and death for a soldier. Their body armor can save their lives as it protects against physical harm. Also, think about when you are going to drive your car, or if you are a passenger, you are required to put on your seatbelt as it will provide some level of protection in case a life-threatening accident occurs. Apply this same principle of using armor to protect yourself from the dangers of overthinking. If you wake up feeling like you are in a constant battle with your mind because you overthink, it is time to learn how to fight back. Do not let another day pass you by where you forget to put on your armor. What is your armor to shield you from overthinking? Your daily habits are your armor; once worn, they can help you become unstoppable. This chapter will teach you what daily habits you should incorporate into your lifestyle to fight back against overthinking. You can still be attacked, even with your armor on, so you must ensure that your armor is designed correctly. Are you ready to craft your armor? Let us proceed to prepare for battle.

Put on Your Armor:

You are here because you have decided that enough is enough, and you are ready to conquer overthinking. You have lost too many moments where you could have been enjoying peace of mind, and you are determined to fight back. Suppose you have recognized that overthinking has become a daily part of your routine. In that case, the only way to fight back is to implement positive daily habits that can overpower your overthinking. These daily habits will become your armor that you use to protect yourself whenever your negative thoughts threaten your mind. I now want to share daily practices that should be part of your routine.

Daily Habits You Can Add to Your Routine:

The Choose Again Method:

The choose again method is an effective strategy that allows you to slow down the momentum built by your negative thoughts and shift your focus by choosing a more positive thought. This method helps you to conquer negative self-talk, in addition to leaving you feeling empowered and allowing you to reclaim your peace. This three-step method requires you first to take notice of your thoughts. Whenever you feel stuck in a negative situation or feelings of fear consume you, it will benefit you to take a step back and examine what is bothering you. The first phase can be achieved by asking questions about how you feel. The second step is to forgive yourself for the thought once you have identified what is bothering you. Even though it may be difficult at first, you can forgive yourself for your negative thinking. The last step is where you choose again, or to put it quite simply, you reframe your negative thought by selecting a positive thought. For example, if you feel nervous over an upcoming interview, this would be the perfect opportunity to tell yourself that you are qualified for the job and that they are interested in everything you have to offer as a prospective employee.

Daily Meditation:

Meditating daily can be an effective method of calming your overactive mind. Meditation helps you to find peace when your mind is racing with constant negative thoughts. To successfully implement meditation into your daily routine, you should start by creating a confident schedule. Frequent practice can make any habit perfect, and meditation is no different. I want you to choose a specific time of day and dedicate that period to meditation, as this will help to train your mind that within this moment, it is now time for your mind to relax. You should always select a time that you are sure you will be able to commit to. Once you have created a schedule, the next step is to find a space that will be your dedicated area for mediation. Your physical environment must be free of clutter or noise and a place of peace and serenity. You can even opt to meditate with others if you prefer. Garone (2021) expressed that "collective energy is a powerful thing, and there is no doubt meditating with a partner or in a class can amplify your experience."

Lastly, meditating does not have to be a dull experience and can be even more successful when you listen to guided meditations that have been pre-recorded. According to Garone (2021), guided meditation is uniquely powerful due to how it impacts your body; more specifically, "This includes activation of the sympathetic nervous system, soothing anxiety, boosting mood, lowering blood pressure, decreasing heart rate, and decreasing the stress response." Now is the perfect opportunity to make your YouTube app your new best friend, as a wide variety of meditation recordings are available. Now that you have identified what you need for mediation, you can begin by incorporating yoga poses as the physical movement will help to stimulate your focus. Then, focus on controlling your breathing to a slow rhythmic pace as this will help to calm your nervous system and help to reduce any anxiety you may be feeling. Your slow breathing is your point of focus and provides relief from your negative thoughts.

Create an Exercise Regimen:

Exercise as part of your daily routine can also help to calm your mind and redirect your focus. Many people have revealed that they can find mental solace when their body is active. As your mind becomes focused on what is happening to your body when you exercise, it provides the opportunity to take a break from your racing thoughts. It might seem obvious and probably does not need to be mentioned, but your mind is an active part of your body, like your arms or legs. However, some view their minds as separate entities from the rest of their physical bodies. This can be problematic as it does not allow you to realize that you must engage and exercise your mind as you do with the rest of your body. Going for a jog or a walk is an effective way to exercise your body and mind.

Affirmations:

Positive affirmations are most effective when you practice them daily, as you constantly substitute your negative thoughts with a powerful and positive affirmation until you believe in it. Whenever you notice that you are overthinking, you can use the following examples of positive affirmations to fight back against your negative self-talk:

1. I am in control of my thoughts, and only I have the power to influence my opinions.
2. Overthinking no longer robs me of my happiness.
3. I am free of self-doubt and any fear that has held me back.
4. I am in control, and I know how to make intelligent decisions.

Breathing Exercises:

I have encountered people who believe the best way to relieve stress and calm their minds is to sit and relax while watching television. Although taking a break can be effective, deep breathing exercises have proven to be more effective. Taking a deep breath triggers a change in emotional and physical state, decreasing muscle tensions and blood pressure. When your muscles relax and your anxiety is normal, your mind relaxes. The best part about breathing exercises is that they can be done anywhere and anytime. We breathe naturally; after all, I am sure you are breathing as you read this book. It is a sign that you are alive and well; however, what you are trying to master is the art of focused breathing. If you were to engage your abdominal muscles while breathing for at least 20 minutes every day, it would help to reduce your stress and anxiety. I sincerely advocate for incorporating breathing exercises as part of your daily habits because "breathing techniques help you feel connected to your body; it brings your awareness away from the worries in your head and quiets your mind" (Marksberry, 2017).

Practice Gratitude:

Even if you are not an overthinker, you should practice gratitude every day as it will allow you to develop an awareness of the positive things in your life that you might have taken for granted. Gratitude can help you to defeat overthinking before it even takes control of you, as you will have naturally developed your appreciation over your life. When you are overthinking and feel anxious about what is going on in your life, it leaves you sad and believing that nothing will work out for the best. Practicing gratitude trains your mind to expect happiness and to see why your life is beautiful and worthy.

Journaling:

When you were younger, did you ever keep a diary that you would hide from everyone else in a secret place? This diary was your safe place to express your fear and true feelings without worrying about being punished or judged. After you wrote down your thoughts in a journal, you felt better, as if your world had become clearer. You might have stopped using your diary once you transitioned into adulthood, or maybe you are one of the limited few that keeps a diary. I bring this up because journaling can be a healthy habit that will assist you in fighting back against overthinking. Writing down your thoughts and feelings can help you to regain control over your emotions. It provides an avenue for you to express yourself healthily, thereby making it an effective tool that can be used to improve your mental health.

When you put your thoughts down on paper daily, you can track what triggers your overthinking and then think of ways to control your mind. You can also use your journal as a forum to identify your negative self-talk and practice positive self-talk instead. Suppose your habit of overthinking has made it impossible for you to make effective decisions. In that case, you can implement journaling as a daily habit as "journaling allows people to clarify their thoughts and feelings, thereby gaining valuable self-knowledge. It's also a good problem-solving tool; often, one can hash out a problem and come up with solutions more easily on paper" (Scott, 2019). If you do believe that journaling is beneficial, well, the proof is in the results as Benton (2022) has revealed that "a 2018 study says that journaling is associated with fewer symptoms of anxiety and depression."

The best way to begin journaling is to start with an open mind and allow your thoughts to flow freely. It may feel awkward at first, but it will come naturally to you after a while, and you will notice how much your mindset has improved. In your journal, you should incorporate a gratitude section where you write down the things you are thankful for in your life. When you stop and notice all the positive things while writing them down, you will eventually realize that your life is wonderful, and there is so much to cherish that you overlook so often because of your overthinking.

Prayer:

Many women have found freedom from overthinking through the power of prayer. Asking God to help you release your fear, worry, stress, and anxiety can help you feel calm, and give you peace that surpasses all understanding. I can't count the times I have been lying in bed at night worrying about my children, money, or my health, and not long after deciding to pray, was able to fall asleep. Prayer does not have to be complicated; it can be as simple as saying "Lord, I am tired, please help me stop worrying and go to sleep." There are many examples of people who overcame overthinking through prayer that can be found in the Bible.

Go Outdoors, Take Photographs:

If you find your mind racing too fast and out of control, taking a moment to step outside each day can help you relax and focus. Observing the beauty of your surroundings can give your mind something more positive to focus on rather than dwelling on whatever negative situation you are facing. Additionally, taking photographs of nature can help you to feel less stress and help to keep you distracted from overthinking. How does taking a photograph help your mind? When you take a photo, you are allowing yourself to be present in the moment and mindful of the beauty surrounding you. Even if it is just for a moment, photography helps to give your mind a break. I want you to conduct your own experiment; whenever you feel stressed or are overthinking, go outside for a walk or a drive with your camera in hand. Even if you do not have a camera, you can also use your phone camera. Take pictures of the birds, trees, buildings, or any landscape that catches your eye. Afterward, take notice of how you feel while reviewing your photos compared to your mental state before you went outdoors.

Overcoming Social Anxiety:

Being afraid of social events, otherwise known as social anxiety, can play a massive role in overthinking. Feeling afraid triggers your body's fight or flight response systems, which can trigger your overthinking. You can overcome your social anxiety if you can identify what triggered it in the first place. You can ask yourself, "which social events make me anxious?" When you arrive at the answer to that question, you can face your fears head-on. What may also assist you is remembering that the relationships you share with your family and friends are a beautiful blessing and may help you feel less anxious. Now that you have a better understanding of social anxiety, you can look at methods to manage your social anxiety and anxiety as a whole.

Treatments to Lower Anxiety:

As you are aware, overthinking can lead to intense feelings of anxiety which is not suitable for your physical and mental health. Treatment for anxiety varies in scope and depends on personal preference. Two less common treatment alternatives that are very beneficial when trying to calm an overthinking mind are acupuncture and massage. Acupuncture is of Chinese origin and is characterized by using tiny needles inserted into your skin at particular points on your body to help stimulate your immune and nervous system. In contrast, a full-body massage can help you to relax and feel less anxious.

Avoid Obsessing Over / Judging Your Thoughts:

You cannot silence your mind completely and obsessing on how to do that can result in even more overthinking. How? Because the more time you devote to trying to stop your negative thoughts, the more they will occur. The opposite of your actions is what will happen. Instead, it would help if you embraced that every human being will have a negative thought at some point, which is a normal part of being human. What you do have the power to do daily is control your negative thinking in specific situations. This can be done by not judging yourself for however you feel or becoming angry at yourself for any negative emotions or thoughts you experience. Acknowledge what you are thinking at that moment and move on instead of fighting with yourself internally. Fight back by loving your mind. Always remember that you will never be able to truly appreciate the role positive thoughts play in your life if you never experience a negative thought. You can also avoid obsessing over your thoughts daily by acknowledging that your perfectionist tendencies are keeping you back. You do not have to be perfect (you will never be), which is quite okay. One piece of advice I want to share, especially with my fellow coffee lovers, is that caffeine can contribute to your anxiety and stress. Although caffeine is not the only problem, you must be mindful of how much you consume. Consuming more than 400 mg daily can leave you feeling anxious and unable to concentrate as you are overstimulated. Let us take a closer look at daily habits to include in your regime to help control your anxiety.

Take Ownership of Your Decisions:

Your decisions belong to only one person, and that person is you. Whenever you make a decision, regardless of the outcome, whether it be positive or negative, you must take ownership for making that choice. Instead of overthinking what you could have done differently, which only increases your anxiety, it is better to accept where you are and what has happened in your life.

Budgeting to Relieve Stress and Anxiety:

We all tend to overthink the state of our financial affairs and doing so can leave you feeling stressed and anxious. Research reveals that "64 percent of adults say money is a significant source of stress in their life" (Young, 2022). Financial stability is a topic of discussion almost every day; therefore, it is helpful to include creating a budget as part of your daily habits to help relieve the stress and anxiety you feel when overthinking your finances. Creating a budget will help create a sense of control within you as it reassures you that your finances are under control. Budgeting could function as a goal that helps you to stay focused and reminds you never to overextend yourself beyond your financial limits.

Therapeutic Alternatives:

Overthinking is not your friend or ally and can leave you unsettled and tired. If you realize, even after changing your methods, that it has not helped to improve your thoughts, you should reach out to someone who can help you professionally. You do not have to seek professional assistance if your lifestyle changes are not working for you, but these things can be used in combination to help you get the best care. Psychotherapy will provide a safe and non-judgmental area to analyze your thinking patterns and identify the root of your overthinking. Two helpful therapeutic alternatives that you can consider are Cognitive Behavioral Therapy (CBT) and Dialectical Behavioral Therapy (DBT). Let us now take a closer examination of each and how they can help you to overcome overthinking.

Cognitive Behavioral Therapy
What Is It?

According to the American Psychological Association (2017), CBT is defined as "a form of psychological treatment that has been demonstrated to be effective for a range of problems including depression, anxiety disorders, alcohol, and drug use problems, marital problems, eating disorders, and severe mental illness." It is one of the most effective forms of therapy, and results indicate that participants experienced a drastic improvement in their overall quality of life.

The Principles of Cognitive Behavioral Therapy:

CBT is based on several fundamental principles, which include:

• Your psychological problems result from your unhealthy or harmful ways of thinking.

• Negative thinking is a learned behavior that is rooted in childhood. Once learned, it develops into Automatic Negative

Thoughts (ANTs), which can be difficult to recognize because they are fleeting. However, you can challenge ANTs by reframing your negative thoughts into positive thoughts.

• CBT is goal-oriented by nature, and the focus is to stop the psychological problem that the participant is facing.

• If you are experiencing psychological problems, you can learn ways to cope and relieve your symptoms.

Cognitive Behavioral Therapy Techniques:

The most common techniques that are used during CBT include:

• The ABC Model

A model which helps you to reinterpret your limiting beliefs. ABC is an acronym for:

Activate the event—what event triggered your negative thinking?

Beliefs—the negative thoughts you had when the event occurred.

Consequences—the negative behaviors that occurred as a result of the event.

• Exposure Therapy

For this technique to work, it requires you to expose yourself to your negative thinking trigger intentionally. The idea is to help you formulate better responses to your triggers.

- Journaling and Role Playing

Writing down your negative thoughts can help you to build a better awareness of your overthinking. Alternatively, you can practice role-playing in potentially harmful situations to help improve how you would respond.

CBT can help you regain control over thinking and integrate strategies that effectively show you how to deal with your anxiety and stress confidently. In order to understand why your stress level has increased, you must identify which thoughts and behaviors contributed to the increase.

Dialectical Behavioral Therapy
What Is It?

Schimelpfening (2021) explained that dialectical behavior therapy (DBT) is considered to be "a modified type of cognitive behavioral therapy (CBT). Its main goals are to teach people how to live in the moment, develop healthy ways to cope with stress, regulate their emotions, and improve their relationships with others." Although it was first designed to treat borderline personality disorder (BPD), it has been expanded to assist in treating other mental disorders. DBT is usually conducted in group therapy, individual therapeutic sessions, or via phone coaching. The primary goal of DBT is to show others how to begin living in the moment, develop healthier ways of coping with their stress, learn how to regulate emotions, and nurture their relationships. The last thing you want is for negative self-talk to take complete control and continue to affect every aspect of your life, including causing you to excessively overthink. When you develop daily habits that help overcome negative self-talk, you can combat your anxiety and feel less stressed.

Dialectical Behavior Therapy Techniques:

• Mindfulness—DBT is focused on teaching people how to develop their mindfulness skills. As discussed previously, mindfulness is based on living in the moment. When you develop mindfulness skills, you also learn to slow down, stay calm, and avoid resorting to ANTs. A sample exercise that is often used to teach mindfulness is to observe your breathing. Observe how your stomach rises and falls as you breathe and note how you feel when you inhale and exhale.

• Regulating emotions—This technique teaches people how to navigate emotions effectively. It begins with naming your emotion and learning to identify and change it. When a person can identify their negative emotion, for example, fear, it will help to reduce the vulnerability they experience emotionally and then help to create a positive memory. The following questions are sample questions designed to help you identify your emotions.

Think of a negative emotion you felt during the previous week, and then describe the following:

1. What event prompted the emotion?
2. How did you interpret the event?
3. What was your emotional reaction?
4. How intense was your reaction (0-100)?
5. What did your emotion communicate to others who were around you? Did it influence their behavior?
6. How did your emotion motivate you to act or respond? What did you do?
7. Did your emotion distort your perspective?

• Behavioral change—DBT also includes strategies that will teach you how to accept your present life situations, your emotions, and yourself overall. Participants can develop the skills they will need to make positive changes to improve their interactions and behavior with others. DBT covers how to analyze your negative behavioral patterns and how they can be replaced with effective alternatives.

Equip Yourself With the Right Weapons:

You have learned about the daily habit that should become part of your armor against overthinking. We will now discuss the issues arising from overthinking and how to protect yourself.

Techniques to Protect Your Health:

Panic Attacks:

The likelihood of experiencing a panic attack drastically increases when you are a chronic overthinker. A panic attack is "an abrupt surge of intense fear or intense discomfort that reaches a peak within minutes" (Burke & Collins, 2012). If you are experiencing a panic attack, as much as possible, you need to remain where you are until it subsides. It is natural to hyperventilate during a panic attack when you take much deeper breaths that leave you feeling dizzy, disoriented, and associated with chest pains. Learning to slow down your breathing will help stop the panic attack.

Furthermore, if you have noticed that before a panic attack, you often feel incredibly anxious, affirmations can be used to lower your anxiety. It would help if you also got into the habit of keeping a written record of what you experience during a panic attack. These tips will help you to identify what triggers your panic attacks and help you to create a plan to treat them.

Insomnia:

If you are overthinking and worry about every detail, it can lead to multiple nights of no sleep. Intrusive negative thoughts make it extremely difficult for you to relax and fall asleep, leading to insomnia becoming your new best friend. If you find yourself struggling to sleep, you can consider CBT as a solution. Another technique you can also consider is the use of imagery distraction. Imagery distraction is when you imagine you are in an interesting scene, such as relaxing on a beach or cooking with family members for a holiday. Once you have selected the image you want, the goal is to immerse yourself into your mental image completely. You want to be able to interact with the sounds, sights, and all the other aspects of a relaxing event. You should avoid creating an extra arousing scenario as this can make you feel even more restless and awake rather than helping you to fall asleep.

For the Moms That Worry:

It is a proven fact that our children are a source of extreme joy and frustration. Having these conflicting emotions can lead to overthinking. Whenever a child is in trouble or pain, it is natural for a parent, especially a mother, to view this as a reflection of themselves and their skillset as a parent. As a parent, you might have noticed that your self-worth becomes influenced by how your child behaves, creating the ideal breeding ground for overthinking. Additionally, the culture of our modern-day society seems to encourage rumination on the part of the parent. All parents ask themselves, "am I doing enough to protect my child? How can I prepare them for the real world?" Social media can add to overthinking, as many negative messages can cause the average parent to overthink and become stressed. Some believe that a mother must be available at all times to provide the best care for development, whereas others promote the idea that daycare is the best solution for the working mom.

So, you naturally end up overthinking, "am I providing my child with everything they need? Am I too strict? Am I making the appropriate choices for the well-being of my child?" Even more unfortunate is that women are usually held primarily responsible for how their children behave. So, whenever something appears wrong, women can fall prey to chronic overthinking or rumination as they believe they have failed as mothers. As a parent, you will always be concerned about your child's well-being—this is an entirely natural aspect of being a parent. It would be best if you did not allow your concerns to escalate until your overthinking leaves you feeling debilitated. The next step is to recognize when you are experiencing the symptoms of parental anxiety; you allow your fears over your child's safety to control your mind. These symptoms usually include the following:

- You try to shield your child from experiencing any type of harm. Avoidant behaviors typically include removing your child or yourself from any situation that appears to be fearful.

- You frequently have conversations about your anxiety and fears over your child, usually with your child in close range so they can overhear what is said.

- You constantly believe that adverse events such as school shootings are more probable to occur rather than being an unlikely possibility.

- You devote all of your time to researching questions about parenting.

Now that you have identified that worrying over your child is natural, you can move on to find relief from this issue before it completely consumes you. Firstly, you need to acknowledge all of your fears and concerns. Then you can work on alleviating those fears by learning about real risks that your children face. Instead of ruminating about what could be happening, you can combat your fear by learning about security measures that are in place for kids if something goes wrong. The deep breathing exercises we discussed earlier can also help calm your mind when you pan out about your child's safety. Anxiety does not have to be a permanent characteristic of your mental demeanor, and there should never be any shame in reaching out for support if needed.

Chapter Reflection

I hope this chapter restores your confidence in yourself and reassures you that you can overcome overthinking. You do not have to let your negative thoughts win the battle, as you can create your suit of armor by simply adjusting your daily habits. Each person will face a different battle and have different factors that trigger negative thoughts. Therefore, the only person that can decide what your armor will look like is you. Your armor will be unstoppable as you are now aware of the various weapons and techniques you can arm yourself with as you prepare to battle overthinking. Worrying about things excessively is harmful and does not help to improve your circumstances. You have to prepare yourself for possible attacks and fight back. Meditation, exercise, deep breathing exercises, affirmations, and practicing gratitude are all daily habits you should make part of your lifestyle to help reduce stress and anxiety. You can also process your thoughts and feelings by writing them down in a journal, or you can go outdoors and enjoy the moment by capturing the positivity surrounding you in a picture. Even if you have been afflicted by issues such as panic attacks, insomnia, or stressing over your children due to your overthinking tendency, you can fight back by using therapeutic alternatives such as CBT or DBT. You are now ready to engage in combat, and you can win the battle against overthinking if you stay focused. If you struggle with remaining focused, the following chapter is for you.

Chapter 5: The Secret to Focus

To conquer frustration, one must remain intensely focused on the outcome, not the obstacles. - T.F. Hodge

Now that you have decided to fight back against overthinking, have you ever stopped to wonder if your ruminating or overthinking is intentional? Do you intentionally focus on the obstacles you encounter instead of the potential positive outcome? Or maybe you have tried to stop overthinking before and found it challenging to stay focused? If any of this sounds familiar, I think it is about time I share a secret with you that I was patiently waiting to let you in on. That powerful secret is the role that staying focused plays in ending overthinking. It all comes down to having clarity in your thoughts. In this chapter, we will discuss techniques to help you to improve your focus. Overthinking leads to procrastination, which leads to indecisiveness and prevents you from being present in the moment. Presence requires concentration, so you must know what could affect your concentration. Let us take a closer look, shall we?

Why Can't You Concentrate?

When you concentrate, you focus on completing a specific activity. The issue is that when you are overthinking, so many thoughts are competing for your attention. There are a variety of factors that can affect your ability to concentrate; let us have a look at some of the primary factors that disturb your concentration:

• Your surrounding environment - This may be a shock for most people, but being in an environment that is too quiet can negatively impact your concentration, just as a noisy environment would. When your surroundings are entirely free of background noise, it can trigger your mind to dwell even more on your negative thoughts. Researchers also discovered that when you are in a cluttered space, your body increases its production of the stress hormone cortisol. When you feel stressed, it is only natural for your mind to resort to overthinking and be unable to concentrate.

• Too many distractions - Distractions are everywhere you go and come in various forms and shapes. One of the biggest distractions in today's modern world is one of our favorite devices, the ever-present smartphone. Tsuei (2022) reported that a study conducted in 2018 proved that the average person would check their smartphone at least every 12 minutes. Constantly checking your smartphone and relying on it for a measure of security can make your overthinking worse. Many had reported that they found themselves doubting their partner based on how quickly they responded to their messages and questioning moments when they seemingly took too long to respond.

• Your mental health—The mental health status can also significantly impact how your brain functions. Mental health complications such as depression or anxiety tremendously influence your ability to remain focused and concentrate. When you are anxious or depressed, it can trigger your mind to overthink as your mind becomes bogged down by heavy thoughts. When faced with these additional mental health issues, it creates additional negative thoughts that only serve as a distraction, making it difficult for you to concentrate.

• Your lifestyle and diet - Your choice of lifestyle and diet also contribute to the quality of your mental health. For instance, if you do not follow an adequately nutritious diet, it can negatively impact your memory and energy level, making it difficult for you to concentrate. Likewise, when you do not get adequate sleep at night, it will make it difficult for you to concentrate on activities the following day. Your lifestyle should include a good night's rest, as poor sleeping habits can develop into insomnia which can trigger your overthinking. In addition to getting enough rest, you should also make exercise a part of your lifestyle choice. Research has proven that at least "30 minutes of moderately intense exercise five times a week can help you think more clearly and boost your memory" Tsuei (2022).

Narrowing Your Focus:

If you are anything like I used to be, you will pick up a book to read, and when you begin to get into it, you decide to pick up your phone or focus on some other distraction that seems impossible to resist. In no time, your reading goal is pushed aside for something else. People have asked: "How do I remain focused when there are so many distractions?" Although this is a critical question for everyone to answer, it is even more important for the overthinker to evaluate. Overthinking is a cunning habit that steals your ability to stay focused away from you. There is hope for you to regain your concentration, as setting goals can help you to become more organized and narrow your focus. You may wonder if any proof exists that narrowing your focus by creating goals works. To answer this question, I want you to think about Steve Jobs and his company, Apple. Do you know what factors contributed to Jobs' success? Apple's profits increased when Jobs decided that the company would focus on manufacturing fewer products than its competitors, allowing Apple to stand out from the rest. Just the same, when you focus on a specific goal, it will help you improve your concentration rather than allowing your mind to dwell on negative thoughts.

So, how do you set a goal? The process of setting practical goals requires you to establish a connection with your values. I want you to pick up your journal and write down your thoughts for the following questions:

• When I think about my life, what things are most important to me?

• What stories inspire me the most?

• What type of behavior makes me feel angry or upset?

• What am I the proudest of in my life?

• During what moments do I feel the happiest?

Digging Deeper: Secrets to Improving Your Focus:

Being unable to concentrate, combined with overthinking, has the unfortunate consequence of making it difficult for you to focus your attention on the positive things that matter in your life. For many of us, concentrating is an arduous task. I have realized that learning to focus is difficult simply because many people do not know the steps they can follow to improve their focus. If this applies to you, I want to help you fix this here and now. Let us now examine methods that will help you learn how to focus and stop overthinking in its tracks.

• Spending time learning to focus—The ability to focus is a learned skill that requires time and effort to master. Look at it this way: when you go to the gym to exercise, you must spend a certain amount of time training your body to get used to a physical regime and develop the muscles you desire. Look at the ability to stay focused as a muscle that you need to spend time working on. The time you spend practicing on remaining focused on a fixed activity will ultimately result in you learning how to remain focused for a more extended period overall. You will eventually improve if you set aside time to practice staying focused and not giving up.

• Setting daily intentions—Setting an intention for every day will help guide and train your thoughts to focus on what it is you intend to accomplish. Your daily intention should be something that you resonate and connect with, as this is what will motivate you to accomplish it. Knowing what you intend on achieving leaves less room for your mind to wander and overthink.

• Overcoming Procrastination—Procrastination is when you delay or avoid taking action on a goal or task you want to achieve. Most people believe that procrastinating is harmless when it can negatively impact your concentration and lead to overthinking. Apart from the factor of self-control, your limiting beliefs, fear of failure, and perfectionist tendencies all contribute to you becoming a chronic procrastinator. The more time you spend dwelling on fear of starting a task or believing that your best is not perfect enough, the more it will decrease your ability to stay focused on what you need to do. You can overcome procrastination by breaking your goals down into smaller steps. Tasks that are too large can leave you feeling overwhelmed and encourage procrastination. When your task is broken down into doable categories, you will notice that you overthink less about what you are doing and can work more productively.

• Using triggers to improve your focus—If you are tired of being unable to focus and stick to your goals, creating a trigger can benefit you. You can design or create a personal trigger that functions as a reminder to act on whatever goal you have in mind. The more your trigger occurs, the more it will lead to you developing a habit of acting on your goal. After some time may not need to rely on your trigger, as your behavior will have become the norm. So, in this instance, if your goal is to stop overthinking about trivial matters, I want you to design a trigger that will remind you to calm your thoughts and focus on something positive instead. Write down your trigger and practice it the next time you find it difficult to stay focused and your mind starts to wonder.

• Taking work break techniques—Sometimes, you become unproductive, struggle to stay focused, and overthink things because you do not take enough breaks. Did you know that there is a way to take a quality break? Firstly, a break must be scheduled. When you do not plan to give your mind and body a rest, it will not happen. You are more likely to end up overworking yourself or feeling guilty and overthinking whether you have worked hard enough. Many have admitted that they do not take a break because they would feel guilty and, as a result, push themselves above their limit. Taking a break can help you to improve your focus and remain productive. Think about it, if you can set your alarm to wake you up, why don't you also set an alarm to remind you when to stop? Regular breaks allow you to have more control over your focus. Scheduling a break is also a form of self-care, as you give your mind enough time to disconnect from your thoughts, and you should notice that you also feel less stressed after a relaxing break.

• Set aside time to worry—One of the reasons why being unable to concentrate and overthinking too much is so harmful to you is because it is heavily grounded in fear rather than finding solutions for the situations you are facing. The less you can remain focused, the more your mind will overthink, which leads to you looking for other situations to worry or stress about. When you add additional problems without finding any solutions, it will lead to your overthinking becoming worse. As you may be aware by now, you will not be able to stop worrying altogether; however, to help you control your focus, you should schedule a time to worry. It may appear counterproductive to some if the goal is to reduce your habit of worrying, but it helps you to worry less. Setting aside time to focus solely on your concerns helps validate your feelings and gives you the power to manage your thoughts and not become stuck in your rumination.

Focus on Your Present and What You Have:

When you overthink, you train your mind to remain stuck in the past or lost in the future. Can you identify how often you sit and dwell on events that occurred the previous day? Dwelling on the past or obsessing over your future denies you the privilege of enjoying being present where you are. It can become far too easy to observe only the negative situations that surround you, as opposed to taking the time to focus on the positive in your surroundings. I want you to truly appreciate your present, as this will help you focus on the things that deserve your attention and not dwell on the negative situations you will never be able to control. Taking advantage of the current moment, close your eyes and inhale deeply, then open your eyes and observe everything around you. When you pause and notice your surroundings, it will become easy to enjoy your present and not let your mind wander to negative things. Living in your present moment also requires you to practice being grateful for everything that you presently have. Let go of trying to overthink about the past and how you can change things and accept your present as it is.

Quieting Your World to Help You Focus:

Although you do not want to be consumed by silence, having the right amount of silence can help you to stay focused and calm your raging thoughts. Learning to quiet the world around you can grant you the power that overthinking stole from you. Cooper (2017) expressed that "silence, perhaps, is our most under-appreciated productivity tool." External and internal noise can be detrimental not only to your physical health but your mental health as well. Research has revealed that people who reside in consistently noisy areas experience an elevation in their stress hormone levels (Cooper, 2017). Silence can help you to shut out any noise that serves as a distraction, so you can improve your ability to focus. With that in mind, let us take a closer look at the importance of silence and how to replace the noise that surrounds you with silence.

The Importance of Silence:

The less focused you are, the more your mind overthinks. It does not allow you to give your mind that much-needed break. Silence helps your mind relax and not feel overwhelmed by your thoughts. In addition to relaxation, silence can help you to think more creatively. One researcher explained that silence could push you towards the pathway of success as "it seems that the capacity to disengage from the outside world when the external environment is sufficiently benign reflects a skill set that is important to almost every human endeavor" (Cooper, 2017). When you are in a place of silence, you can unplug and disconnect from all negativity. When you can relax and disconnect, you will also feel more patient. An overthinker is more likely to feel frustrated and impatient, especially when they struggle to stay focused. Silence can help you to cultivate an atmosphere of peacefulness and calm that will allow your thoughts to slow down.

Decision Making and Overthinking:

When you overthink constantly, you may have noticed that you find it exceedingly difficult to make effective decisions regarding the aspects of your life that genuinely matter. To build on this point, when you lack focus, you either become distracted or put off making important decisions that can create more significant issues. Neither scenario is ideal for anyone, and so both should be avoided. If you can control the thoughts cluttering your mind, you can also make efficient and effective decisions. I want to share with you some methods to help you learn how to make smarter decisions and not allow overthinking to impede your decision-making abilities. These methods are:

1. Choose a mission or goal and stick to what you have chosen.

2. Decide a time frame or limit that will help you focus on the decision that needs to be made. Adding a timer can help you address your situation's roots with a reduced risk of becoming distracted.

3. Avoid exposing yourself to decision fatigue by ignoring trivial decisions and focusing only on important ones.

4. Decide which decisions are trivial or essential by focusing on situations you can control instead of things outside your direct control.

It's Okay if You Make a Wrong Decision:

I can personally tell you that absolutely no one enjoys feeling as if they have made a wrong decision; especially when there is a lot at stake because of the decision that they have made. Overthinking whether you have made the right choice will not benefit you in the long run, either, and will only leave you feeling anxious or stressed as you dwell on the outcomes of your decision. There is only one plain truth when it comes to decision-making: at one point or another, all of us will make a wrong decision. Making wrong choices is a natural, unavoidable part of life and can help you learn what not to do in the future. So, if you realize your decision was not the best at any point, there is no need to beat yourself up over your choice. Instead, this is where you should practice self-care and be self-compassionate. Even though you may feel as if your choice will cost you, it can teach you an invaluable lesson. So, what if you went over your savings budget for the month? Instead of judging yourself for not being perfect and overthinking how you have now set yourself back financially, you should recognize that you made a mistake, which is quite okay. You can focus on doing better the following month.

Chapter Reflection

In this chapter, we analyzed how and why overthinking is not intentional thinking. Being intentional requires having clarity of thought and making intelligent decisions for yourself. The greater your ability to stay focused and be present in the moment, the more control you would have over your overthinking. To help you learn how to focus, it is imperative that you first learn about the factors that can affect your ability to concentrate. Your surrounding environment, diet, and mental health can all work together to prevent you from concentrating. However, all is not lost, as narrowing your focus by establishing your goals can help you to improve your concentration.

Likewise, learning how to set aside time to worry and taking a regularly scheduled break will make a difference in how you stay focused. You also should not underestimate the value of silence, as quieting the world around you can help you to feel calm and reduce how much you overthink.

Furthermore, being unable to focus can also impair your ability to make the best decisions for yourself. Once you can learn how to focus only on the important decisions while accepting that it is okay and normal sometimes to make a wrong decision, you should notice an improvement in how you feel and think. Learning to love yourself can make a difference in your focus and overthink. The following chapter will take a closer look at what loving yourself means.

Chapter 6: How to Love Yourself Well

It's a funny thing about life, once you begin to take note of the things you are grateful for, you begin to lose sight of the things that you lack. –Germany Kent

When you overthink, you tend to devote a lot of your time to contemplate your past, present, future, or even hypothetical situations that have not yet occurred. You may even notice that you replay conversations you previously had with someone so frequently in your mind that you begin to attach a negative meaning to some of their words. These combined activities can contribute to self-doubt and low self-esteem, which triggers overthinking. It is time to direct your attention to the role of self-esteem and negative self-talk. I want to ask you a couple of questions first. When you think about yourself, do you describe yourself as an unsuccessful or socially awkward person? What are some words you use to describe your personality or the mistakes you have made in the past? The things you say about yourself may not even be accurate, but you have convinced yourself to believe your negative reviews because of your overthinking.

Here is another question that I want you to answer honestly. Can you remember when a friend or family member has done something embarrassing or made a mistake? I am sure that the answer is "of course not," and neither will they be able to recall every error you have ever made. Our mistakes are mostly forgotten or go unnoticed. However, the overthinkers, especially those who have a perfectionist mindset, are always conscious of every error or event that hasn't occurred and beat themselves up about it. You end up spending most or all of your mental energy dwelling on things you have no control over. For example, you have an interview in a couple of days, yet you spend all of your time ruminating about how you will be unsuccessful at the interview. When you talk negatively to yourself, it can ultimately serve as a type of self-fulfilling prophecy. Repeating negative comments to yourself influences how you act and feel about a situation, making it more likely to occur.

So, in this chapter, I want to discuss how self-love can be used as a tool for breaking yourself free from negative self-talk and overthinking. Loving and accepting yourself for who you are is imperative before any other strategy to conquer overthinking can work. I will begin by discussing negative self-talk and how to identify when you are engaging in this unhealthy behavior. I will also share with you a variety of methods that can be used to overcome negative self-talk and teach you how to love yourself more.

Identifying Negative Self-Talk:

One factor I have learned along the way is that most people tend to overthink the aspects of their self-image to which they have attached negative labels. After all, the more confidence you have in yourself, the less reason there will be to worry. Likewise, instead of overthinking your past mistakes, you will view them as catalysts for your growth and believe that you can prevent errors from occurring in the future. It all comes down to how you look at yourself and talk to yourself. Beau-Shine (2021) emphasized that when it relates to self-talk, "the way we communicate with ourselves plays a major role in the way we see and experience the world around us. That's why being mindful of these delicate words we use regularly is extremely important." However, I want to reassure you that it is entirely normal if there are times when you let negative self-talk get the better of you. It has also happened to me multiple times, but what made the difference in my journey was becoming mindful of when I was engaging in negative self-talk. To begin becoming aware of when negative self-talk is happening, let us first get a clear definition of what it is.

Self-talk is considered a mental skill primarily concerned with the type of statements we make to ourselves. Self-talk can either be positive or negative, with the ideal type being positive, as this influences our notions of self-worth and, ultimately, how we perform. Have you ever heard a voice inside your head whispering to you that you are not good enough? Or perhaps this voice said that you would never be able to achieve your goals? Or maybe you have an upcoming exam or meeting, and that voice has told you that you will fail? That negative voice is your mind engaging in negative self-talk. One perspective that stands out was provided by Scott (2018), who explained that "negative self-talk is any inner dialogue you have with yourself that may be limiting your ability to believe in yourself and your abilities and to reach your potential." Internalizing and believing in these negative statements decrease your ability to make the positive changes you want to see in your life. So, if you tell yourself that you will never break free from the chains of overthinking, the outcome will be that it will affect your confidence in your ability to achieve your task. You do not want this to happen, so it is essential to recognize the different forms of negative self-talk.

Forms of Negative Self-Talk:

Four primary forms of overthinking can occur: catastrophizing, personalizing, polarizing, and filtering. Let us take a brief look at each of these, so you can identify if you engage in any of the above-listed categories.

Catastrophizing:

If you recall, you encountered this word earlier in a previous chapter. To summarize, catastrophizing falls under the category of negative self-talk as it involves you mentally anticipating the worst outcome in any given situation. Even when there is no indication that the worst will occur, you believe it will or has already happened. This type of self-talk can be controlled when you ask yourself questions such as "is this likely to happen?" It would help if you also challenged yourself to think about other possible outcomes rather than ruminating on what you believe will occur.

Personalizing:

This type of self-talk is characterized by you automatically placing the blame on yourself whenever something goes wrong. With this attitude, you live by the mantra "it is my fault, not yours." For example, you are messaging a friend and notice that they take much longer than usual to reply to your messages. You instantly start telling yourself that they are angry with you or do not want to be friends anymore when perhaps they could be busy and unable to respond immediately.

Challenging your thoughts is the best way to avoid this type of negative self-talk. Ask yourself, "why am I thinking this way?" and then try thinking of alternative reasons that can counteract your negative thinking.

Filtering:

With filtering, you will find yourself completely filtering or leaving out all the positive aspects of a situation to instead focus solely on the negative. I am sure many people can admit to an example of filtering, myself included. You create a monthly budget to help grow your savings, and after one month, you end up going over your budget. The way filtering works is that you focus on the one month over budget instead of acknowledging the other months when you have been able to meet your savings goal. Regardless of your accomplishments, the negative will always outweigh the positive.

Polarizing:

Under this category of negative self-talk, you typically find yourself with two perspectives: bad or good, with no in-between or middle ground. One example that can help to illustrate this type of self-talk would be to say that you have been arriving at work on time every day and meeting all your deadlines. However, one morning you arrived late, so you could not complete one of your work reports on time. Because of this, you begin telling yourself that you are a lazy person or a failure. Polarizing does not leave room for making mistakes; instead, you label yourself under one fixed category.

What Can Cause Negative Self-Talk?

Now that we have identified the types of negative self-talk, it will also benefit you to understand what can cause negative self-talk. One of the first reasons why you may engage in negative self-talk could be because you spend far too much time socially isolating yourself away from others. Spending time around others allows you to distract yourself from negative thoughts, thereby limiting your negative self-talk. Spending too much time alone can worsen your negative self-talk when you refuse to ask others for help. For some people, when they feel stuck in their cycle of negative self-talk and overthinking, they choose to bottle up their feelings instead of asking for help, which only makes things worse. Another factor that can trigger negative self-talk is not setting aside enough time to practice self-care. Just as taking care of your physical health, your mental well-being is equally important. When you neglect taking care of yourself, it gives negative self-talk the perfect opportunity to increase. Furthermore, spending too much time around negative people is one way of ignoring yourself. When you associate with negative people, the outcome is that it increases your negative self-talk.

Overcoming Negative Self-Talk:

How to Identify Your Thought Pattern:

I want you to be able to take control over your negative self-talk, and this requires you to be able to identify your pattern of thinking. When you identify your thought process, you will become more familiar with how your self-talk adversely affects you. To help you accomplish this, I have some activities that I want you to complete. For the first activity, I want you to take your journal and list the thoughts you experience the most often. After you have identified these thoughts, I want you to reflect and write down how these thoughts have affected you, your career, and your family. The second activity is designed to help you identify and replace the negative statements you say to yourself. List some of your negative beliefs about yourself and challenge yourself by replacing them with positive statements.

Self-respect is the first of many tools you need to equip yourself with to nip negative self-talk and, ultimately, overthinking in the bud. The only person that can identify the inner critic that is preventing you from showering yourself with love and care is none other than, you guessed it, You. That inner voice that has been saying many harmful and hurtful things to you, most of which you would never say to someone else, must be silenced. I know how overwhelming it can be to replay these negative statements about yourself, or surrounding situations, over and over in your mind. It is frustrating, and to be truthful, it can be very harmful. Your negative self-talk is what limits or inhibits you and prevents you from pursuing all of your goals. Negative self-talk strips you of your peace of mind, and this, my dear reader, is what you need to overcome. I want to clarify one thing before we proceed any further. You will not be able to remove negative self-talk altogether. What you do have the power to do is control it and how frequently it takes control over you. If you can limit the number of negative statements you make, you will notice that you spend less time overthinking. It all begins with learning to love yourself more.

The Role of Self-Respect:

Now that you have gained a better understanding of negative self-talk, I want to direct your attention to a term you should familiarize yourself with. That term is *self-respect,* a complete game changer when breaking free of the chains of overthinking. I want you to begin with some self-interrogation and ask yourself what does respect mean to you and why does it matter? Write down your answer and return to it after reading this chapter. Firstly, I want to begin by answering the question of self-respect and why it matters. Gepp (2022) explains that self-respect involves "loving yourself and treating yourself with care. It's the result of staying true to your values and not being willing to compromise." When you engage in negative self-talk, you undermine your self-respect, allowing your negative thoughts and feelings to overshadow your values and best personal traits. The more you engage in negative self-talk, the more you overthink, and the harder it is to have a positive outlook.

Self-respect is the best representation possible of self-care. The more you can practice positive behaviors that are consistent with your values and beliefs, the more confident in yourself you will feel. The first step in showing yourself self-care and learning to love yourself requires you to develop and practice behaviors that demonstrate self-respect. You can begin to build self-respect by establishing what your values are and why they matter. Values are the beliefs that you deem essential in your life. Examples of values can include commitment, loyalty, or integrity. You can define your values by asking yourself, "what is it you value the most in your life?" Then ask yourself if your thoughts are helping you to be closer to your values or if they are taking you further away from them. The goal is to help you identify the positives in your life, and what matters to you, as this will help you stay focused on your objectives instead of dwelling on the negative aspects around you. If self-respect means taking care of yourself, you must uncover what care involves. Do you know what your needs are and how to satisfy them? Or are your needs not being met because of your thoughts?

Learning to Love Yourself More:

If you have ever felt alone and you believe that no one else understands how difficult it can be at times to fall in love with yourself, I want to acknowledge your feelings by letting you know that you are not alone. Loving yourself can be difficult, as it takes a lot of work and mental fortitude to appreciate your own worth. You may have been trained to believe that you need affirmation or validation from others, and this inaccurate belief can contribute more to negative self-talk. When someone else cannot validate you by saying that you are beautiful or good enough, it can shape your thoughts about yourself, which you may find yourself dwelling on. When you do not love yourself, you become more critical of who you are, and your negative self-talk deepens. You can improve and love yourself by first recognizing when you are engaging in self-sabotage.

Negative self-talk IS self-sabotage, as you use your own thoughts to destroy everything unique and excellent about you.

Earlier, I asked you to write down what self-respect means to you and why it matters. I want you to build on this by analyzing what words you say to yourself to show yourself love and respect. Above anything else, the words that you say to yourself matter. If you notice that the statements that you make about yourself aren't positive, then this is the area that you need to improve. You can avoid sabotaging your mind by using positive affirmations.

Positive affirmations grant you a particular type of control wherein if you believe what you say; you can achieve it. So, precisely what are positive affirmations? Affirmations are statements or phrases that you repeat daily to yourself to help you overcome self-sabotaging your mind with fear and self-doubt. When you find it challenging to show self-love, especially during complex events that encourage your negative self-talk, positive affirmations are a personal and powerful tool to counteract those negative thoughts. Simply put, you can shut down negativity and show yourself some much-needed tender loving care by affirming yourself. The great thing about positive affirmations is that you can construct them to suit your personal needs or concerns. For example, whenever you are catastrophizing and assuming that the worst outcome is about to happen, you can control your thoughts by using a positive affirmation such as "I know that I am strong, and I can handle anything that I face." Affirming your strength helps you feel less anxious over the negative possibility and more validated by your power.

Other positive affirmations could be to tell yourself, "I know that this situation will be difficult, but I also know that I possess the skills needed to handle every situation." You can design how your affirmations will flow, and they will help you to acknowledge the factors that triggered your negative overthinking. Most importantly, positive affirmations enable you to believe and respect yourself. I recognize that it will take some time to get used to repeating positive affirmations, but you can become more consistent with daily effort. Take the time every day to repeat at least one positive affirmation to yourself, either out loud or silently. Even if you struggle initially to develop a routine of using affirmations daily, you must remember to practice self-compassion. Be mindful and sympathetic that you are learning a new habit; it will take some time to break down the limiting beliefs already in your mind. Negative self-talk and overthinking do not develop into habits overnight and using positive affirmations will not either. It will require focus and commitment; are you ready to make a start? If you are, you also need to be aware that at the beginning of this process, you may find it easy to doubt yourself, which is entirely normal.

Practice Self-Acceptance:

When I refer to the term self-acceptance, I am referring to your ability to embrace everything about yourself without having any form of condition or expectation. Self-acceptance means that you have accepted both your positive and negative qualities. You cannot love yourself if you only accept the excellent facets of who you are; you must be able to embrace any negative aspects as well. It is a well-known fact that the biggest struggle facing most people is learning to accept themselves. This struggle becomes even more significant for an overthinker as they tend to ruminate on their failures or fear being rejected or judged by others. When you throw a perfectionist mindset into the mix of things, it becomes complicated for an overthinker to accept the possibility of making a mistake or the potential for failure at any point in their life. Overthinkers who are perfectionists lack self-acceptance and are most critical about themselves. This type of mindset is what will keep you back from enjoying the life that you always wanted. I want you to think about it for a moment; have you truly accepted yourself for who you are? Are you comfortable in the environment that surrounds you? Do you even know how to begin accepting yourself when you have become used to ruminating?

One of the best places to start your journey of conquering overthinking is to begin with self-acceptance. The way change works is when you devote your time to trying to be someone you are not, you're more likely to remain stuck in that loophole. Therefore, you will understand genuine change if you learn to accept everything about yourself. After you have acknowledged your less-than-perfect traits or characteristics, the ability to change your self-talk and mindset from negative to optimistic will come more naturally to you. You need to fall in love with the principle of unconditionally accepting yourself. When I say unconditionally, I mean you must be able to accept yourself at all times and not only during moments of self-doubt or when you find your thoughts are racing and you surrender to overthinking. You must accept yourself during periods of victory and at your weakest or lowest moments. Unconditional self-acceptance means that you have come to understand that your mistakes will never define you, as it is natural for you to be imperfect and make mistakes.

The trick to mastering self-acceptance is learning to empower yourself and not judge yourself critically. I am sure that in the past, you were able to identify habits about yourself that you desperately wanted to change, and you judged yourself for having those habits. For example, you probably picked up this book because you recognize you are an overthinker and are tired of allowing your thoughts to control you. Maybe you judged yourself harshly in the past when you realized that you were overthinking.

To overcome overthinking, you must first embrace that you are an overthinker. Once you have accepted this is your habit, you can focus on embracing the other positive qualities you have instead of only dwelling on the negative. You can't overcome overthinking if you refuse to accept it as part of your identity. You must embrace it, be compassionate towards yourself, and only then will you set yourself on the right path towards conquering overthinking.

Chapter Reflection

In this chapter, we took a deeper look at what it means to love yourself and the role it plays in helping you overcome overthinking. True self-love requires you to identify when you are engaging in negative self-talk. This is when you make negative statements about yourself that affect your self-esteem and overall self-image. The more you engage your mind with negative words, the more opportunities you have to ruminate or overthink them. These statements only serve one purpose; they hinder your ability to reach your true potential. Your responsibility is to control your negative self-talk by practicing self-care and respect. Take the necessary time to identify your values and goals and what they mean to you. Above all, you must accept yourself and all your good and bad qualities.

The methods I shared with you in this chapter are meant to help you grow to love and accept yourself for the long term. Although it may take some time for you to bear the fruits of your labor, you can rest assured that it will result in you having a greater sense of personal control over the quality of your thoughts. As reiterated throughout this chapter, self-love can only begin with you. It would be best if you held yourself accountable for the action plan you started. What do I mean by holding yourself accountable? In chapter 7, we will learn more about accountability and how it can be used as a method for breaking free of overthinking.

Chapter 7: Accountability:

Holding Yourself Accountable

Wisdom stems from personal accountability. We all make mistakes; own them... learn from them. Don't throw away the lesson by blaming others. - Steve Maraboli

I once heard an expression in which overcoming overthinking was compared to being able to free yourself after becoming trapped in quicksand. Taking back control of your thoughts can be challenging. The last step I want to discuss with you to break free from overthinking involves taking accountability for yourself. Responsibility is critical as it grants you the power to put an end to your self-defeating thoughts. Throughout my years of research, I've discovered that true success is achieved when you take full responsibility for the course of your actions. Throughout this book, you should have learned how to identify the roots of your overthinking, your triggers, and the factors that allow you to remain stuck in this negative loop. By taking accountability for the nature of your mindset and holding yourself responsible for overcoming overthinking, only then will you be able to break free truly. In this chapter, I will discuss accountability's role in helping you achieve your goal. I will also offer tips that will assist you in finding an accountability partner who can help you to remain focused on your journey of breaking free from overthinking.

The Meaning of Accountability:

When you hear the term accountability, what words immediately cross your mind? For me, the first word that always pops up is responsibility. One of the most straightforward definitions of accountability is a personal willingness or obligation to take responsibility for our actions. For some, accountability is regarded as "taking ownership" (Judge & Open Textbook Library, 2012). The only way to change your negative habits of overthinking is if you assume responsibility for your thoughts and hold yourself responsible for setting goals to break free. You DO have the power to change your thoughts from negative to positive as "constructive change and learning is possible when accountability is the norm" (Judge & Open Textbook Library, 2012).

I want to ask you a question you may have never been asked. The question is, "who are you accountable to?" (NC, 2020). Record your answer if you have been making notes in your journal thus far. You may even find yourself surprised by the answer. Another question you should ask, especially if you have tried before to overcome overthinking, is, "do you know why it is so important that you hold yourself accountable for the outcome of your actions?" To state it much more simply, "accountability leads to success. Taking responsibility for your actions makes way for the changes that lead you to do things differently. It can mean doing new things or not doing things that have held you back" (NC, 2020). From this perspective, you should realize that if you have yet to take accountability and hold yourself solely responsible for shifting your mindset and thinking positively, this character flaw keeps you back.

Setting Yourself Up for Success:

The more challenges you face daily, you may feel a significant risk of falling back into your habit of overthinking. It may even feel as if you can only temporarily switch off that voice of worry and doubt. The thing is, you are always going to face conflicts or rejections. Taking responsibility for how you respond to these events can help to reduce the likelihood that life's challenges will send you spiraling downwards into the pit of overthinking. Accountability can be your powerful personal tool that helps to place you on a successful path towards achieving your goal of conquering overthinking. So, this leads to the next question that I am sure you are eager to have answered; "how can accountability benefit me?" Well, let us examine some of the benefits of accountability:

- Holding yourself accountable can drastically impact your progress towards achieving your goal of conquering overthinking. The idea is to connect with someone who shares the same goal as you, so you can obtain the feedback you need on your performance. When you receive guidance and reviews regarding your routine, it can help you build confidence that you are taking the steps in the right direction.

- Accountability allows you to measure your progress and success. I want to briefly mention the term accountability partner, as we will discuss the role of this person a little later on in the chapter. This partner or mentor will help you to define what success will look like for you. Everyone has a different perspective on success; it can't be measured on a scale. For example, success for one person may be to stop dwelling on why they haven't found a spouse yet, whereas, for another, success could be learning how to let go of their past and accept where they currently are in life. Accountability will help you to measure how much progress you have made in achieving these visions of success.

- If you genuinely want to let go of overthinking as a habit, then you must be engaged in achieving this goal. Here is where accountability steps in and allows you to stay engaged and not lose interest or forget about why you have been working so hard. Of course, it is only natural to become distracted along the way. It happens to the best of us. However, because holding yourself accountable allows you to keep a record of your progress, it can give you the drive you need to keep working towards your goal.

• The factor that I admire the most about taking accountability for your actions and thoughts is it helps instill a sense of responsibility. When no more excuses are being used as to why overthinking is impacting your life, it allows you to take steps that you must implement in your life to reach where you want to be. Accountability provides the critical lens of analysis that shows you how success is in your hands and nobody else's.

Accountability Ladder:

So, you have decided that you are tired of feeling stuck, anxious, or simply overwhelmed by the amount of time you spend living in your head, and you have made the conscious decision to put an end to your habit of overthinking. Accountability is the practice of taking responsibility for your patterns and answering for the outcomes of your decisions. Bowen (2015) expressed that "once we accept the fact that our actions have consequences, we are empowered to make the effort that creates the results we want." Pause for a moment and reflect on what results you want to see in your life. Do you know what accountability should look like for you? The last thing you want at this stage of your progress is to feel like a victim of overthinking. Instead, accountability should leave you feeling empowered, as if you are moving up the ladder of success.

The first stage of empowerment is acknowledging your reality by admitting to yourself that you are aware of your habit of overthinking, but this is not your permanent reality. Victims are usually unaware of the problem or have no goals to solve their issues. That is where one may usually blame and complain to others about what they are going through. Accept ownership of your thoughts if you find yourself constantly replaying the same idea repeatedly. Acknowledge what you are feeling, and do not make excuses. Instead, find a way to embrace the nature of your thoughts and solutions to what has triggered your actions. Nobody else can control your thoughts and emotions or decide how you respond to situations. You are responsible for doing the inner work, assessing your mindset, and making the changes you want.

Accountability Starts with Self-Examination:

Accountability can only start with you and you alone; therefore, you must take a good look at yourself. You can do this by reflecting on your past situations. Be truthful and examine how things could have turned out differently if you were to take responsibility for how you thought about the situation. I want you to identify your actions to avoid being held accountable; did you deny, shift blame to someone else, or outright refuse to accept any responsibility? You need to examine your past behavior because it will help you determine the roots of your inability to assume accountability. There could be various reasons; however, the most common factors are arrogance, a fear of being judged by others, or a lack of self-confidence. Now that you have identified your triggers and causes, you can move on to a useful method to help you assume accountability: finding an accountability partner.

Accountability Partners:

Lean on Others:

Talking to a trusted friend, spouse, or family member has proven to be a popular and effective method of overcoming overthinking. One of the main reasons I have discovered why people are motivated to lean on others is that it helps them to feel understood and accepted during challenging moments. Another reason is that it helps people sort through their thoughts and arrive at better decisions. For example, you argue with your partner and decide to turn to a close friend to discuss what happened. Your friend might be able to ask questions that will help you to get to what triggered your negative reaction. They might also help you uncover positive responses that you can use to help rectify the situation that you are facing instead of ruminating about what has already occurred. To put this into a better perspective, let us look at Carla's story.

Carla knew immediately that she had to talk to someone about her problem. She'd had a terrible argument with her husband, Christopher, that escalated into Christopher asking her for a divorce. Although it had seemed obvious that their marriage was in trouble for some time, his declaration of divorce left her completely stunned. As she proceeded to complete her daily errands, she found it extremely difficult to take her mind off the argument that had taken place earlier that morning. She also found herself replaying previous fights and analyzing every single word that had been said before. Her overthinking was not helping her, so to ease her mind, she decided to pay her best friend, Susan, a visit. Susan was one of the few people she felt she could always seek advice from to help her calm down and think more clearly. They had attended the same college together and had been married for almost the same length of time. Susan asked Carla to explain what transpired during the argument and to identify what she felt were the biggest obstacles in her marriage. They spent the next few hours talking, and by the end of the conversation, Carla noticed that she felt calm, affirmed, and overall supported by her friend. Susan had promised to recommend a trusted marriage counselor and check in on her friend to see how she was adjusting emotionally.

As you can observe from Carla's situation, her friend Susan was able to help her remain calm when she began to overthink excessively and assist her in regaining control over her thoughts. The role that Susan played is the essence of what an accountability partner is. Having an accountability partner makes some people feel as if they are doing something wrong, and they can't take control without any assistance. However, this perspective is entirely inaccurate. The role of an accountability partner is to provide a reliable support system grounded in trustworthiness and honesty. Your accountability partner is responsible for checking in on your progress, identifying your next steps, and applauding your accomplishments. Whosoever you choose as your partner must be someone that you can be completely honest with about your thoughts. You will surely notice the difference in your progress if you select your accountability partner wisely. Let us now shift our attention to learning what an accountability partner is and how having one can benefit you.

The Role and Benefits of an Accountability Partner:

If you are struggling to create a new habit, for example, maybe you are trying to think more positively and worry less, then an accountability partner can be your person who assists you in achieving this task. To describe an accountable partner, Ho (2020) explains that this person "is someone working solely to keep us in check and accountable. There can be more than one person who will keep you focused and committed to your goals and ensure that you take the right steps to success." Learning new habits can be daunting, and it might help you to feel affirmed and supported to know that there is someone genuinely interested in seeing you improve. This relationship is a mutually agreed upon partnership in which both parties agree to act as mentors and provide feedback within a specified timeframe.

Sometimes, as human beings, we all need that extra push to help us attain our goals. One of the primary benefits of having an accountability partner is that it allows you to create a bond with another person who also shares similar goals or struggles. I can personally attest to feeling embarrassed to admit to someone else that I am guilty of overthinking. However, with an accountability partner, it creates a forum of complete vulnerability, free from judgment, because of mutual understanding and trust. Your accountability partner can also help to keep you motivated. Losing motivation happens to everyone, and you shouldn't feel ashamed if this has happened to you. The critical point is that losing motivation can hinder your real progress towards achieving your goal. I've noticed, and perhaps you have also, that people tend to give up on their goal entirely once they have lost motivation. This is where an accountability partner can step in and take charge. They can help you to stay motivated via their actions and words. Trust me when I say that the right words from a trusted person can make a huge difference in developing a new habit. Your accountability partner should not give up on you whenever you feel demotivated; instead, they should encourage you and remind you why you embarked on this journey.

The ability to motivate another person to achieve success is a beautiful thing to witness. It is also lovely to see someone overcome a habit they thought they would never break free from. Feedback is one of the criteria that can help you to be aware that you are progressing steadily in your journey. Honest and unbiased feedback is often tough to obtain. One of the reasons it is so difficult to get is that you may surround yourself with friends or family members who feel terrified that they might hurt your feelings, so they avoid telling you the complete truth. Keeping people around you who cannot give you honest feedback will not help you break your habit of overthinking. Feedback will distinguish failure from success, and an accountability partner provides honest feedback.

Finding the Perfect Partner:

I now want to share the qualities of an efficient accountability partner and how you can build your relationship with them. You must be able to find the most suitable partner as you do not want to be around someone who will make you feel down. If you are now wondering what qualities you should keep an eye out for in an accountability partner, let us look at the following:

1. They are disciplined.

Discipline is a quality that would benefit us all, not just accountability partners. When people are disciplined, they can motivate others and help them avoid procrastination. The proper discussion with your accountability partner can help you to recognize when you are falling back into your overthinking habit and push you back on track.

2. They know how to challenge you.

You need a partner that does not accept mediocrity as an outcome but instead challenges you to improve yourself. An accountability partner knows how to get you to work harder and stop doubting your abilities.

3. They are patient and supportive.

Sometimes you may feel as if you lack the self-confidence or courage needed to change how you view the problems or situations you encounter daily. An accountability partner must recognize that it is natural to feel doubtful when trying something new, so they are patient with you. Breaking free of overthinking will not occur overnight, and your partner shouldn't rush you to make decisions. Instead, having a partner available to provide words of encouragement and support will benefit you the most. Your accountability partner must always have your best intentions at heart.

4. They know how to provide constructive criticism.

The value of constructive criticism is often overlooked in all relationships. Criticism is usually perceived negatively; however, the focus should be on the word "constructive" rather than criticism. Constructive criticism is the ability to provide direct feedback without making the person directed feel down or embarrassed. An accountability partner skilled at giving constructive criticism will be able to address your concerns without breaking your spirit.

Creating an Accountability Statement:

One method you can implement into your partnership with your accountability partner to ensure that you are on track to achieving your goal of breaking free from overthinking is to create what Ho (2020) labeled as "weekly statements of accountability." To explain how an accountability statement works, Ho provided the acronym PACT, which stands for:

P—possible

A—action-based

C—clear

T—time-bound

Possible: When you think of your overall goal to break free of overthinking, are the smaller goals that you have created feasible or easy to attain? For any goal to be possible, you must be able to complete daily tasks that will help you to reach your goal.

Action-based: The other question you need to be able to answer is whether you can act on or execute your goal. For instance, if your goal is to stop worrying about the past in one month, then that is impossible as there is no action specified on how you can achieve it. A stronger accountability statement would be, "I will list five positive things that occurred every day of the month." This statement emphasizes the plan of action you will follow to achieve your goal.

Transparent: Your accountability statement needs to be as concise and straightforward as possible. You should include factors that can hinder your goal when writing your statement.

Time-bound: Your accountability statement should specify the timeframe you expect to achieve your goal. You should keep in mind that setbacks will always affect your ability to achieve your goal by the expected deadline. In that case, the deadline is just to keep you focused, rather than feeling overwhelmed that you must meet the specified date.

Getting Started with Your Accountability Partner:

I want you to give yourself a round of applause for doing the work needed to conquer overthinking. You chose to hold yourself accountable for your life; without action, the knowledge that I am sharing with you becomes pointless. Celebrate your tiny victories with your accountability partner. One of the biggest challenges many face is learning to open up to others, especially family, about their issues. Instead of initiating a sudden conversation, plan ahead by choosing where and when you want to have your discussion. If you can plan what you would like to discuss, this can help you to feel more comfortable and relaxed. Write down your core thoughts that have been bothering you and explain how you feel from your perspective. Acknowledge what you feel and clarify what you need help with. Allow your accountability partner to help you and return the favor by listening and sharing ideas. Accountability partnership helps create meaningful relationships as you use your shared goal to help each other.

Chapter Reflection

We have covered a lot of ground in this final chapter. Here is a brief overview of what we discussed in this section: I introduced you to the concept of accountability and how it can make a positive difference in your life. Accountability, also known as taking ownership, is an effective method to help you overcome your battle with rumination or overthinking. It is your primary responsibility to always protect yourself, and you can accomplish this by beginning with a complete self-evaluation of your mindset. Indeed, we have seen that it is only natural at times to feel overcome by your thoughts and emotions when facing a difficult situation, but you do not have to allow overthinking to claim your entire life. So, how do you become successful at breaking free of overthinking? You do so by holding yourself accountable for your thoughts, as this act of accountability will allow you to observe your progress towards breaking free of this destructive habit.

Furthermore, you do not want to surround yourself with people who will pull you down even further into the trap of overthinking. Instead, you must eagerly seek out and lean on others who share the same personal goal of overcoming overthinking and who can challenge you rather than contribute to your downfall. This type of person is known as an accountability partner. Your accountability partner must be someone with whom you can honestly confide your thoughts and with whom you can be completely vulnerable. An effective and efficient accountability partner must provide genuine support and display specific characteristics: honesty, self-discipline, and patience. Additionally, your accountability partner should challenge you to meet your goal, provide constructive criticism, and work with you to develop mutual accountability statements. This will enable you to remain motivated to succeed at breaking free of the habit of overthinking that once consumed you.

$100 AMAZON GIFT CARD CHRISTMAS GIVEAWAY

Follow the QR code link below to enter.

Conclusion

I am in complete awe of you as you have reached the end of this book. I sincerely hope you will be able to practice the techniques you have learned and truly master the ability to avoid overthinking. Life can be overwhelming at times. Overthinking can leave you feeling exhausted and, for some, depressed. You have the power to propel yourself out of that negative well and onto a positive path of self-love and self-improvement. The most significant obstacle standing in your way is your mind, as change must come from within. The only remaining advice I can share with you at this final stage is to revisit the sections of this book that stood out the most to you and use a highlighter to mark those sections. This way, whenever you feel you are taking steps backward instead of moving forward, it will be easy for you to return to the section that assisted you with overcoming the issue you are facing. This could also be something you pass down to your children if they struggle with overthinking sometime in the future.

Time to Recap

Let us take a moment to look back at the lessons we have learned in this book: Chapter 1 examined the roots or causes of overthinking. Then in chapter 2, we addressed the depth to which overthinking can affect our lives and the importance of becoming aware to avoid spiraling downwards and becoming stuck in the Dwell Well. Our mindsets play an integral role in determining how we interpret and feel about our lives, which is why in chapter 3, we focused on getting started by learning how to shift our mindsets. We looked at the role of mental blocks and limiting beliefs, being able to identify them, and methods to overcome them. We also addressed the role of perfectionism, the need for control, and how to overcome those habits. Chapter 4 addressed how we can fight back against overthinking by practicing daily routines such as mediation, exercise, or affirmations. You also learned how to equip yourself with techniques that will help you identify your triggers and address health issues that arise from overthinking. Chapter 5 brought forward techniques we can all use to improve our focus and concentration and rewire our brains to spend less time overthinking. Chapter 6 addressed the importance of loving yourself to overcome overthinking. Finally, chapter 7 discussed accountability's role in overcoming overthinking and the incredible benefits you can enjoy if you find an accountability partner.

Moving Forward

Examine your progress daily, from where you started to where you are now and feel proud of yourself. In everything you do, the key to success depends on your consistency and determination. The methods I have shared with you will not take effect overnight, but with the right attitude and time, you will notice the difference in your life. I am praying for you and genuinely believe that if you take the sincere time to practice the journaling activities and self-reflecting exercises provided within this book, then you can and will find victory over overthinking. Above all, you must believe in yourself and trust in your mind's power. I also have one small request for you that will allow you to assist other readers who would be interested in finding and benefiting from this book. It would mean a lot to me if you could leave a review on Amazon and share your feedback with me. I read every review and I am so grateful for your time spent leaving a review.

References

American Psychological Association. (2017, July). *What is cognitive behavioral therapy? American Psychological Association.* https://www.apa.org/ptsd-guideline/patients-and-families/cognitive-behavioral

Anderson Witmer, S. (2021, July 12). *What is overthinking, and how do I stop overthinking everything?* - GoodRx. GoodRx. https://www.goodrx.com/well-being/healthy-mind/how-can-i-stop-overthinking-everything

Beau—Shine, A. (2021, June 13). *4 science-backed ways to identify and stop negative self-talk.* Fast Company. https://www.fastcompany.com/90645945/4-science-backed-ways-to-identify-and-stop-negative-self-talk

Benton, E. (2022, April 26). *How to use journaling for stress relief.* Psych Central. https://psychcentral.com/stress/how-to-begin-journaling-for-stress-relief#takeaway

Bowen, J. (2015, December 15). *How accountability leads to success.* Jan L Bowen. https://janlbowen.com/how-accountability-leads-to-success/amp/

Burke, D., & Collins, D. (2012, July 5). *Panic disorder.* Healthline; Healthline Media. https://www.healthline.com/health/panic-disorder

Charlie. (2022, May 20). 30 *most common things to overthink and why we do it.* 107.5 Kool FM. https://1075koolfm.com/most-common-things-that-people-overthink/

Cooper, B. (2017, February 2). *The power of silence: Why you need less noise for work and your health.* Zapier; Zapier. https://zapier.com/blog/silence-health-productivity/

Definition of overthink. (n.d.). Www.merriam-Webster.com. https://www.merriam-webster.com/dictionary/overthink

Felman, A. (2020, March 12). Stress: *Why does it happen and how can we manage it?* Www.medicalnewstoday.com. https://www.medicalnewstoday.com/articles/145855

Focus quotes (1541 quotes). (n.d.). Www.goodreads.com. Retrieved June 22, 2022, from https://www.goodreads.com/quotes/tag/focus

Garone, S. (2021, April 2). *9 Tips for meditating when you're an overthinker. Healthline.* https://www.healthline.com/health/mind-body/9-tips-for-meditating-when-youre-an-overthinker

Gepp, K. (2022, March 21). *Self-respect: What it is, how to achieve it, and why it's important.* Psych Central. https://psychcentral.com/blog/how-to-improve-self-respect#how-to-improve-self-respect

Get out of your head! 81 overthinking quotes to ease your worries. (2021, December 13). Scary Mommy. https://www.scarymommy.com/overthinking-quotes/amp

Ho, L. (2020, January 22). *How to build new habits with an accountability partner.* Lifehack. https://www.lifehack.org/862621/accountability-partner

Javier, N. (2021, June 3). *Here's how overthinking is affecting your personality.* The Bridge Chronicle. https://www.thebridgechronicle.com/lifestyle/self-optimisation/heres-how-overthinking-is-affecting-your-personality#:~:text=But%20even%20without%20that%2C%20overthinking

Judge, W., & Open Textbook Library. (2012). *Focusing on organizational change.* Open Textbook Library.

Love yourself quotes (428 quotes). (n.d.). Www.goodreads.com. Retrieved June 22, 2022, from https://www.goodreads.com/quotes/tag/love-yourself

Marksberry, K. (2017, January 4). Take a deep breath- The American Institute of Stress. *The American Institute of Stress.* https://www.stress.org/take-a-deep-breath

Moore, K. (2015). Rumination and self-destructive thoughts in people with depression. *Behavioural Sciences Undergraduate Journal*, 2(1), 5–12. https://doi.org/10.29173/bsuj281

Moore, K. (2017, November 17). *How to overcome mental blocks.* Monday.com Blog. https://monday.com/blog/productivity/5-helpful-tips-overcoming-mental-blocks/

Most women think too much, overthinkers often drink too much - UM News Service. (2003, February 4). Ns.umich.edu; The Regents of the University of Michigan. http://ns.umich.edu/Releases/2003/Feb03/r020403c.html

Murdock, J. (2020, July 15). *Humans have more than 6,000 thoughts per day, psychologists discover.* Newsweek. https://www.newsweek.com/humans-6000-thoughts-every-day-1517963?amp=1

NC, K. S. (2020, January 6). *5 Reasons Accountability is important for success.* Provision Nutrition. https://www.provisionnutrition.net/single-post/2020/01/06/5-reasons-accountability-is-important-for-success

Overthinking quotes (146 quotes). (n.d.). Www.goodreads.com. https://www.goodreads.com/quotes/tag/overthinking

Schimelpfening, N. (2021, November 5). *What to know about dialectical behavior therapy.* Verywell Mind. https://www.verywellmind.com/dialectical-behavior-therapy-1067402

Scott, E. (2018). *How to reduce negative self-talk for a better life.* Verywell Mind. https://www.verywellmind.com/negative-self-talk-and-how-it-affects-us-4161304

Scott, E. (2019). *Is journaling an effective stress management tool?.* Verywell Mind. https://www.verywellmind.com/the-benefits-of-journaling-for-stress-management-3144611

Tredgold, G. (2016, June 1). *49 Quotes that will help you avoid the blame game*. Inc.com. https://www.inc.com/gordon-tredgold/49-quotes-that-will-help-you-avoid-the-blame-game.html

Tsuei, J. (2022, March 2). *Tips for how to improve concentration and focus*. Clockwise. Www.getclockwise.com. https://www.getclockwise.com/blog/improve-concentration-tips

Wiseman, E. (2017, September 8). *There's a scientific reason why you're always overthinking everything*. Grazia. https://graziadaily.co.uk/life/real-life/women-active-brains-overthinking-study/

Young, C. (2022, January 12). *5 Reasons budgeting is good for health*. EverydayHealth.com. https://www.everydayhealth.com/emotional-health/why-making-a-budget-can-be-good-for-your-health/

My Daily Habits Tracker:

	Meditation	Exercise	Affirmations	Breathing Ex.	Gratitude/ Prayer	Journaling	Go Outdoors
S							
F							
Th							
W							
T							
M							
S							

My Daily Habits Tracker:

	S	F	Th	W	T	M	S
Meditation							
Exercise							
Affirmations							
Breathing Ex.							
Gratitude/ Prayer							
Journaling							
Go Outdoors							

My Daily Habits Tracker:

	Meditation	Exercise	Affirmations	Breathing Ex.	Gratitude/ Prayer	Journaling	Go Outdoors
S							
F							
Th							
W							
T							
M							
S							

My Daily Habits Tracker:

	S	F	Th	W	T	M	S
Meditation							
Exercise							
Affirmations							
Breathing Ex.							
Gratitude/ Prayer							
Journaling							
Go Outdoors							

My Daily Habits Tracker:

	Meditation	Exercise	Affirmations	Breathing Ex.	Gratitude/ Prayer	Journaling	Go Outdoors
S							
F							
Th							
W							
T							
M							
S							

My Daily Habits Tracker:

	S	F	Th	W	T	M	S
Meditation							
Exercise							
Affirmations							
Breathing Ex.							
Gratitude/ Prayer							
Journaling							
Go Outdoors							

Gratitude Journal - I'm Thankful For:

1.

2.

3.

4.

5.

6.

7.

8.

9.

10.

Gratitude Journal - I'm Thankful For:

1.

2.

3.

4.

5.

6.

7.

8.

9.

10.

Gratitude Journal - I'm Thankful For:

1.

2.

3.

4.

5.

6.

7.

8.

9.

10.

Gratitude Journal - I'm Thankful For:

1.

2.

3.

4.

5.

6.

7.

8.

9.

10.

Gratitude Journal - I'm Thankful For:

1.

2.

3.

4.

5.

6.

7.

8.

9.

10.

<u>Gratitude Journal - I'm Thankful For:</u>

1.

2.

3.

4.

5.

6.

7.

8.

9.

10.

Affirmations:

I am free from stress.

I release the past and accept the future.

My mind is at ease.

I am

_____.

I love

_____.

I release

_____.

I have

_____.

I forgive

_____.

I receive

_____.

I am

_____.

I celebrate

_____.

I release

_____.

I attract

_____.

Affirmations:

I am

_____.

I love

_____.

I release

_____.

I have

_____.

I forgive

_____.

I receive

_____.

I am

_____.

I celebrate

_____.

I release

_____.

I attract

_____.

Affirmations:

I am

_____.

I love

_____.

I release

_____.

I have

_____.

I forgive

_____.

I receive

_____.

I am

_____.

I celebrate

_____.

I release

_____.

I attract

_____.

Affirmations:

I am

_____.

I love

_____.

I release

_____.

I have

_____.

I forgive

_____.

I receive

_____.

I am

_____.

I celebrate

_____.

I release

_____.

I attract

_____.

Affirmations:

I am

_____.

I love

_____.

I release

_____.

I have

_____.

I forgive

_____.

I receive

_____.

I am

_____.

I celebrate

_____.

I release

_____.

I attract

_____.

Notes:

Notes:

Notes:

Notes:

Notes:

Notes:

Notes:

Made in United States
North Haven, CT
15 November 2022

26774964R00109